The Japanese and the Jews

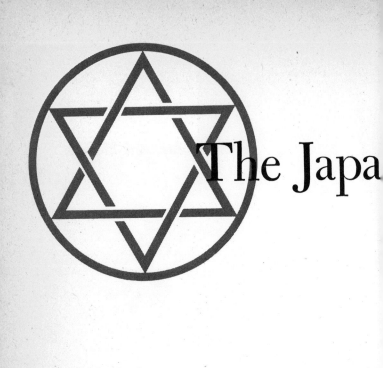

The Japa

nese and the Jews

by ISAIAH BEN-DASAN

translated from the Japanese by
Richard L. Gage

New York · WEATHERHILL · *Tokyo*

This book was originally published in Japanese in 1970 by Yamamoto Shoten, Tokyo, under the title Nihonjin to Yudayajin (The Japanese and the Jews).

The design used on the binding, title page, and chapter-opening pages shows the Star of David imposed on the Rising Sun. The six-pointed star, however, is also an ancient Japanese family crest called kagome (basket weave); this has been adduced in support of the theory that some of the remnants of the lost tribes of Israel eventually settled in Japan.

First English edition, 1972
Third paperback printing, 1983

Published by John Weatherhill, Inc., of New York and Tokyo, with editorial offices at 7-6-13 Roppongi, Minato-ku, Tokyo 106, Japan.   Copyright © 1970, 1972 by Yamamoto Shoten; all rights reserved.   Printed in Japan.

LCC Card No. 72-78951   ISBN 0-8348-0158-2

Who is wise? He who can learn from every man.
Who is mighty? He who can control his passions.
Who is rich? He who is satisfied with his lot.
Who is honorable? He who honors mankind.
> —Ben-Zoma (in the *Mishnah*)

He whose deeds exceed his wisdom, his wisdom shall endure; but he whose wisdom exceeds his deeds, his wisdom will not endure.
> —Chanina Ben-Dosa (in the *Mishnah)*

Let it not enter the mind that anything in the world's system will cease to exist when the Messiah comes, or that any novelty will be introduced into the scheme of the Universe. The world will go on as usual.
> —Maimonides

Contents

	Translator's Note	*ix*
1	The Cost of Security	*3*
2	Animals Sacred and Profane	*27*
3	The Fangs of Cronos	*41*
4	Villa People, Highway People	*57*
5	Politics Abstract and Pragmatic	*71*
6	Divine Law, Human Law	*95*
7	Unique and Exclusive	*105*
8	A Martyr to Nihonism	*119*
9	Contractual and Parental Deities	*133*
10	Peoples Without Virgin Births	*141*
11	Persecution in the Offing	*153*
12	Some Misconceptions	*167*
13	Abacus and Formula Thinking	*177*

Translator's Note

A famous writer once defined the translator's duty as presenting in another language the exact content—absolutely no more and no less—of the original. This sounds easy, and it would be if all the translator's work were on the level of *la plume de ma tante*. It rarely is, however, and translating serious writing inevitably involves the re-creation of a microcosm produced and conditioned by a specific language, the historical background of the users of that language, and the personality of the author. On all three counts, a literal translation of *The Japanese and the Jews* was almost impossible and free adaptation imperative.

Although many Western readers are familiar with the history of the Jews, the number conversant with the history of Japan is much smaller. Ben-Dasan is lavish in his use of illustrative materials from Japanese culture and history, both of which he knows extraordinarily well. But, though figures like Saigo Takamori are as well known in Japan as

Napoleon is in the West, the uninitiated Occidental reader must have assistance if he is to follow the author's analysis of the Japanese experience. For this reason, materials have been added when it was felt essential to do so.

Ben-Dasan has written his book in the purest Japanese idiom. Since Japanese and English are so vastly different that even translating simple materials directly can be difficult, I have striven to give the author's meaning without trying to reproduce exactly his distinctive and utterly Japanese style.

The personality of the author is very special indeed. A Jew born and raised in Japan, he understands the Japanese perhaps better than they do themselves. Nowhere is his grasp of the Japanese spirit more apparent than in the literary form in which he has cast his materials. He has written what is best described as a Nihonist essay because this is the form that would best reach his Japanese audience. Since Western readers accustomed to Aristotelian logic would find Ben-Dasan's Nihonist reasoning startling if it were not adapted to a certain extent, I have made appropriate changes. By and large, however, the work retains its fundamentally Japanese—that is, Nihonist—cast and flavor. The author borrowed this Japanese way of viewing many aspects of life fundamentally for the sake of revealing to the people of Japan interesting facets of their national character. But both his method and his material have much to offer the Westerner, too. Accept the Nihonist essay on its own terms without attempting to force it into Western patterns of logical thought, and you will find it novel, fresh, and meaningful.

The treatment of Japanese names in this book follows a now

well-established policy. I have used the Western order—surname last—for all people born in the modern period of Japanese history; that is, after 1868. For all people whose lives predate this era, I have used the traditional Japanese order—surname first.

The Japanese and the Jews

1. The Cost of Security

THE COMPARISON IMPLICIT IN THE TITLE of this book requires some explanation. I am the first to admit that few peoples are as fundamentally dissimilar as the Japanese and the Jews. Indeed, readers who know one or the other of these peoples intimately may perhaps object that any comparison is impossible. As a Jew born and raised in Japan, I know both the Japanese and the Jews well, and I am only too keenly aware of the difficulties involved in comparing them if the aim of the examination is to discover similarities. There are simply too few to bother hunting for them. Moreover, I believe that the only meaningful comparisons are those that attempt to find and analyze differences. By discovering wherein one entity differs from another related one, it is possible not only to learn much about both things, but also to draw certain broad conclusions about the general class to which they belong. In short, by turning the light of inquiry on the distinctive traits of the Japanese and the Jews I think I can illuminate their national personalities while simultaneously shedding a ray or two on some interesting aspects of humanity.

In this initial chapter I have chosen to begin by contrasting the attitudes of the Japanese and the Jews toward the vital issue of security. As my discussion progresses it will become apparent that the need for security does not stop at safety-deposit boxes or even national-defense establishments but extends into the deepest places of the human heart. A desperate search for safety during the long ages of the Diaspora has influenced every phase of Jewish life, while relative ignorance of the cost of security has done much to mold the Japanese mind. Because particulars are more vivid than generalities, I shall attempt to illustrate this point with an anecdote that a friend once told me.

Some time after the end of World War II and while anti-Japanese feelings were still running high in the United States, Japanese business concerns began sending representatives to major American cities to reestablish trade and business connections that had been severed during hostilities. One such representative was a man I shall call Suzuki —a pseudonym as common and imaginative as Smith— who was assigned to the New York area. Perhaps he mistook the New Yorkers' natural coldness for hostility, or perhaps they were in fact not inclined to be gracious to a former foe. In any case, Mr. Suzuki felt himself very oppressed by the cold shoulders and hostile glances that seemed to greet him everywhere. This upset him so much that he gradually came to regard his hotel room—he was staying at an expensive mid-Manhattan hotel—as his only haven of peace and safety.

In the room next to his there lived an elderly Jewish couple, and Suzuki struck up an acquaintance with them, since they seemed to harbor no anti-Japanese feelings. As the days and weeks passed, Suzuki came to be on an almost family footing with the couple and was able to observe them closely. He noticed that they were unpretentious and unostentatious in their activities. Their clothes were good but not flashy. In the dining room they ate modestly and drank little. "But surely," thought Suzuki, "if they can afford to live permanently in an expensive hotel like this, they must be rich." His friends' apparent frugality suggested that perhaps the old stories about Jewish parsimony had some basis in fact.

One day his curiosity got the better of him and he asked point-blank: "Why do you live here? It costs a great deal more than a nice house in the suburbs. If you had your own house, you could live in a better style for less. Why throw your money away like this?"

The question did not seem to surprise the elderly couple, but the husband's reply astonished Suzuki: "It may seem old-fashioned to you, but we live in this hotel for the most important of all reasons—personal safety. You see, although things are much better now, we remember some ugly moments in our neighborhood in the thirties when anti-Semites were on the rampage. I don't mind saying that we were badly frightened. And we decided then and there that safety is the most important thing in life. After all, what good is a big bank account if your throat's been slit? So we moved in here where we've got doormen, guards, and house detectives to protect us. It costs more than we'd like to pay, but at least we're safe."

This way of thinking completely baffled Suzuki, as it

would any Japanese: never having been forced to pay for security, the Japanese cannot imagine that such a condition could be possible. Though some people in Japan also choose to live in hotels, it is only out of a desire for convenience or luxury, never because of fear or the desire for safety. Sometimes, when labor agitators demonstrate in the streets before their houses at all hours of day and night, Japanese company presidents have been known to move with their families to hotels—simply to get some sleep. But neither they nor any other Japanese have ever regarded a hotel as a fortress of safety.

Giving the matter more thought, Suzuki began to wonder if his Jewish friends were not only fanning the flames of anti-Semitism and prejudice by remaining aloof from other people. On one occasion he put this point to them, and once again their answer opened a whole new field of thought to him. They said that no matter where they are, Jews are always isolated from the society around them, because they inevitably must live in one or the other of two kinds of ghettos.

But perhaps this is enough of Suzuki and his friends. Suffice it to say that in time Suzuki came to realize that his friends were in fact old-fashioned in their thinking, that their fears were more typical of the hate campaigns of the troubled thirties than of the circumstances of Jews in America today. Nevertheless, what they told him about the two Jewish ghettos did illuminate certain aspects of Suzuki's own country, where the very concept of the ghetto is all but nonexistent.

It was Theodor Herzl, the founder of modern Zionism, who first pointed out that there are two kinds of ghettos, the inner and the outer. The most obvious and infamous kind is the physical, outer ghetto like those of Warsaw and other eastern European cities. Since he lived before the horrors of Nazism proved him partly wrong, Herzl could say that Jews who remained in their own settlements—that is, within their ghettos—were reasonably safe and spiritually free. On the other hand, a Jew who left the ghetto and became assimilated into society at large by attempting to give up his Jewishness gained physical liberty but forfeited spiritual freedom. Sometimes described as the epitome of the assimilated Jew himself, Herzl knew what he was talking about. He had fully experienced the black wall of secrecy and pretense that is the inevitable fate of the assimilated Jew. To describe the state of mind bred by this pretense, he used the term "inner ghetto," which means self-imposed spiritual bondage accepted for the sake of physical freedom.

Herzl may have coined the phrases, but the inner and outer ghettos have been with the Jews for a very long time. During the Middle Ages, large numbers of Jews elected to live in the inner, spiritual ghetto by ostensibly renouncing Judaism and becoming Catholics. The practice was especially widespread in Spain and Portugal, where converted Jews were known as Marranos—a term that later came to be applied to converted Jews throughout Europe.

I myself am a descendent of Marranos, and I have studied their history in some detail. Most of them skillfully deceived the watchful eye of the Church. In fact, there is a tradition that a famous Catholic saint was actually a Marrano. Nor would it be especially surprising to find that the story is founded on truth, for the Marranos went to great lengths to prove their allegiance to Rome. To demonstrate their fervor and thereby protect themselves from persecution as Jews, they made enormous financial contributions to churches and monasteries. In this way they resemble Suzuki's elderly Jewish friends, who paid huge hotel bills for the sake of safety.

But no matter how well the Marranos concealed their Jewishness, in time many of them were found out and subjected to punishments of revolting cruelty. Slow roasting over hot coals was one of the less excruciating tortures to which they were put. Consequently, knowing the fate that awaited them if they were unmasked, at the slightest sign of danger the Marranos would abandon everything they owned and flee. Some went to Palestine, feeling that if they must die anyway the historic home of Jewry was the best place for death. Others escaped to Venice, the New York of the Middle Ages, or to England and many other countries, always searching for the safety that stayed forever beyond their grasp.

In seventeenth-century England, during the turbulent days of Puritan control under Cromwell's Protectorate, Jews were persecuted less severely than were the hated Catholics, or Papists, as the Puritans called them. No matter what their nationality, Catholics were rounded up and tried and severely punished. At that time a certain Spanish Marrano named Antonio Rodrigues Robles was living in London. He fell into the Puritan net and was put on trial. Under questioning, however, he claimed that he had only pretended to be a Catholic and that he was actually a Jew, a Marrano, whose true allegiance was to the ancient faith of his fathers and not to Rome. At a loss for what to do, the presiding magistrates applied directly to Cromwell, who is said to have ordered the man freed.

Robles was lucky. While in Spain, he had saved his life by choosing the inner ghetto of pretended Catholicism, and then in England he saved himself once again by retreating into the outer ghetto of Judaism. Not many Jews in history have been able to accomplish such a double switch. Most of them have been faced with a single choice between the inner or outer ghetto, and never has the choice been an easy one.

Religious persecution throughout the ages has forced Jews to understand that security does not come free. It must be paid for one way or another. And what about the Japanese? For them the situation is almost entirely the reverse. Suzuki's reaction was typical when he found it difficult to grasp the reality of his Jewish friends' situation: neither he nor most of his countrymen have had any experience with religious persecution.

Only once in Japan's history did a situation arise in which some few Japanese were compelled to seek protection in something like an inner ghetto. In the sixteenth century, Christian missionaries from the West made many converts in Japan, but later, for political more than religious reasons, the Japanese government strictly proscribed the new religion and issued edicts that any Christian who refused to give up his religion should be deported together with his family. Thereafter, anyone found to be secretly practicing Christianity would pay with his life. As I have said, historically the Jews have usually been able to choose between the inner and the outer ghetto, but the Japanese Christian who wanted to remain in Japan had no choice other than the inner ghetto. There were no colonies to which he could emigrate in order to practice his own faith unmolested. Had the Japanese government set aside some remote zone where the Christians would be safe so long as they did not venture out into the rest of society, then the Japanese converts would have been faced with the painful choice between inner and outer ghettos. But this did not happen. The choices were simple: deportation, which a few elected; apostasy, with or without retreat into the inner ghetto; or death, which many suffered for their faith. And over the centuries of being cut off from the Church, even the inner ghetto all but faded away, so much so that there were only a few thousand secret Christians still living in Japan when the nation was finally opened to intercourse with the world in the late nineteenth century.

This then, together with a very small population of the so-called Eta, or outcastes, who traditionally have lived in their own communities, constitutes Japan's sole and very insignificant experience with ghettos of any kind. It is entirely correct to say that the whole ghetto concept is completely outside the experience of the average Japanese.

Many Westerners seem to think that the Japanese were first granted true freedom with the introduction of democracy by the American occupation forces after World War II and that they do not yet understand the value of this freedom that was so generously bestowed upon them by a victorious enemy. This is patent nonsense. Having lived for many years in prewar Japan and studied Japanese history deeply, I can say flatly that the Japanese have always lived in complete freedom from the kind of inner and outer bondage I am discussing here. Social pressure, yes, this they have had in plenty—and what nation has not? And the Japanese have also had more than a good share of enforced political conformity. But at the same time they have almost always had one of the most important of all freedoms—the freedom of security. The Jews, on the other hand, have almost never had security. Over the ages, persecution has forced countless Jews in many lands to flee their homes. In our own time, this has happened on a tragic scale in eastern and central Europe; and it continues to happen today, as recent events in the Soviet Union make painfully clear. In contrast, never in their long centuries as a nation have the Japanese had to flee their homes in search of security. To be sure, some few have emigrated to the United States and to South America, but their objectives have been wealth and success, not a search for security.

In short, with a list of exceptions too brief to do more than strengthen my assertion, the Japanese have always known complete security. The result of this blessing has been that they find it incomprehensible that security should cost money. To them, safety, like water, is free to all men. They know nothing of waterless deserts and the hopeless craving for even a drop of the precious liquid.

Later I shall have more to say on the subject of the contrasting natural environments of Japan and Israel, but the comparison of security and water is so pertinent to the present discussion that I shall pursue the point a bit further here. Israel is an arid land where every drop of water is extremely valuable, whereas Japan enjoys heavy rainfall and torrents of sweet water from mountain rivers and melting snows. Similarly, whereas the inhabitants of Israel, since ancient times, have had to develop extensive irrigation systems—such as the famous ones of Jerusalem and Megiddo—until recently the simplest methods of rice-paddy irrigation have sufficed for the Japanese. Besides needing complicated equipment and facilities for providing water, the Jews also had to devise sewerage systems to rid their cities of refuse and thus protect themselves from epidemic diseases; while the Japanese, surrounded by vast stretches of sea and ocean, have—at least until modern urbanization changed the situation—simply allowed their rapidly flowing rivers to flush waste matter into the sea, where it vanished quickly and harmlessly. Water, then, is highly valued and closely guarded by Jews and taken completely for granted by Japanese.

The expense and difficulty involved in building the great waterworks of Jerusalem and Megiddo were if anything overshadowed by the immense cost of building the famous walls of Jerusalem. But the expense could not be avoided because, from the Jewish viewpoint, the security provided by the walls was imperative and, like water, was to be obtained only by dint of great effort. The Japanese approach, however, is quite different, as indicated by a remark of a famous sixteenth-century Japanese warrior named Takeda Shingen: "Human beings are the castle, they are the stone ramparts, they are the moat; compassion is the ally, feuding is the enemy." Certainly Shingen himself never built a castle, and even though others did build them in Japan, it was only to protect the interests of the ruling class, not to repel a foreign invader; and no Japanese anywhere ever entertained the idea of surrounding an entire city with protective walls. What was there outside to be protected from?

I do not mean to suggest that Japan's entire history is one of halcyon bliss. War and strife aplenty have plagued the nation, but in comparison with the fate of other parts of the world, the bloodshed and fighting the Japanese have known amount to little more than squabbles between closely related clans. For instance, never have the Japanese experienced anything comparable to the fate of Paris during the Hundred Years' War. At one point during that grim period, battle casualties and the Black Death reduced the population of the city by half. Both the dead and the living dead—those who, though infected, were living but were treated as corpses—were hauled in vast numbers outside the city, where packs of hungry wolves waited to devour them. Only the city walls protected the miserable few who managed to survive, much as the hard shell protects the vulnerable body of the oyster.

Or to give another example that is even more to the point, neither have the Japanese ever experienced anything like the fate of Jerusalem in A.D. 70, when Titus and his Roman armies held it in siege for two years. All of the efforts of the Jews to withstand the mighty war machine of the Romans and to sneak food into the city through intricate tunnels proved futile. In the end the great Temple itself was burned, the city was reduced to rubble, and thousands of Jews were sold into slavery. The walls of Jerusalem, which had cost the Jews so much in labor and expense and for so long had given them security, were destroyed. But ultimately even the conquerors had to rebuild them, for protection has long been uppermost in the list of essentials for the cities of both Europe and the Near East, even as it was the reason for the building of the greatest wall the world has ever known, the Great Wall of China.

But the Japanese have never built city walls: protected by the sea from outside invasion, they have felt no need of them.

On a more homely level, the Japanese rarely resort to the use of sturdy locks and keys. Indeed, the concept of locking up is so little developed among the Japanese that they have never felt the need even to distinguish between a lock and a key, the single word *kagi* being used to designate either object in the Japanese language. The formality of locking up before going to bed is often ritually observed, but the thin doors, the flimsy locks, and the very structure of the traditional Japanese house could not possibly deter a thief seriously intent on burglary. When I was a child in Japan, I often saw families sleeping out of doors in summer with no more protection than a mosquito net, and in all probability their front doors had been left unlocked behind them.

People who require a collection of locks and chains on their apartment doors or those who live in cities where women remove their jewelry before going out at night for fear of being robbed cannot possibly understand this carefree attitude. But it is part and parcel of the Japanese mind. No matter whether the issue is the walls of a city or the safety latch on a door, the Japanese attitude is that steps taken for the sake of security ought not to cost anything because such steps are unnecessary; in short, no device or means of security is worth the candle.

Whether before or after World War II, the Japanese have never regarded the military forces or the police as the true guardians of national and personal security, to be paid for by public taxes and hence to be ultimately responsible to the public who pays them: they are simply other unnecessary security measures, the luxurious whims of a willful government. A famous political thinker named Yukio Ozaki put the fundamental Japanese position succinctly

when he said that military forces in peacetime are as use-
ful as an umbrella on a sunny day.

The mass media today continue to argue along the same
lines. When flood or avalanche suddenly strikes and the
Self-Defense Forces rush to the rescue, the papers applaud
their efforts but also take the occasion to add that, since
Japan is now a nation of peace, emergency relief is about
all the military can be expected or desired to provide. In
fact, the prevailing attitude is that the existence of the
military represents virtual tax theft on the government's
part, and journalists cry outrage when hefty allotments
are made for the purchase of fighter planes or other military equipment. All official efforts fail to convince the people that a modicum of preparedness in the military line is
essential in this modern world. Physical safety and freedom
from ghettos of all kinds are the rights of Japanese and
therefore ought to cost no more than water.

As I have already observed, Japanese history is far from
being one long golden age of peace. No more are the Japanese totally free of fear. The things that the Jews fear
scarcely need defining in a century that has witnessed what
this one has. Surely the very mention of a word like genocide strikes all compassionate people hard enough to make
the meaning of Jewish fear blood-chillingly clear. The
Japanese too have their list of deadly fears, but it is re-
markably lacking in the horrors of plague, genocide, discrimination, persecution, and, until recently, war. The
Japanese dread sudden, unpredictable, uncontrollable natural calamities and, having had so little experience with
them, are much less concerned about the disasters caused
by man. Their list of frightening things, as often given in
their traditional literature, goes thus: earthquake, thunder,

fire, and the Old Man. A brief examination of these fears will shed some light upon Japanese psychology.

Of the four things most feared, the most terrible is earthquake, for it comes totally without warning and wreaks some of the most tremendous havoc known on earth. The Great Kanto Earthquake of 1923 caused more damage in Tokyo and Yokohama than did all the holocaust of atomic bombs in Hiroshima and Nagasaki. Moreover, unlike the case of earthquakes, the possibility of being attacked with some sort of superweapon was not entirely unexpected. After all, the Japanese had been told often enough of the marvelous inventions their own forces had just in the offing, and being the pragmatists they are, they could hardly have thought their enemies would have more scruples than themselves in using whatever new means of destruction came to hand.

As for thunder, it is known and feared the world over, whereas only certain areas are subject to earthquakes. Dogs and children crawl under beds at thunder's horrible crack, and everyone has heard tales of the blinding bolt and the shattering roar that strike down the unwary traveler. In Japan, as elsewhere, thunder is associated with a number of folk beliefs and superstitions, but it is also thought of as a symbol of all the natural elements in their uncontrollable fury, especially of the typhoon. In this symbolic sense, thunder ranks second among the four fears because the annual devastation to agricultural crops caused by storms and typhoons exceeds that of all other disasters.

Until only recently Japan was a land of almost exclusively wooden architecture. It is scarcely to be wondered then that third in the list comes fire. In a crowded city of flimsy buildings, a small, initially localized fire can quickly spread over large areas, leaving nothing but smoke and ashes in its wake. So frequently were large areas of Tokyo destroyed by fire in the past, especially when that city was still called Edo, that the wry humor of the townspeople dubbed fire "the flower of Edo."

The last of the fears, the Old Man, represents authority as vested in some patriarchal figure. The idea originated in the traditional Japanese family structure, in which the husband-father, as undisputed head of the family, had final say in all matters. He was feared because of the limitless power he wielded, but he was also revered as the pillar supporting the entire structure of the family and, by extension, society as a whole. Since so much of Japanese society is patriarchal in tone, the Old Man figure plays a vital role outside the family as well, beginning with the role of the emperor as the father of the nation. The Old Man also becomes the gang boss or the company president or the shop foreman, all of whom have traditionally exerted dictatorial power over their underlings. And to an extent, national leaders and politicians become Old Man figures too as they handle the weighty matters of government. The Japanese have a profound aversion for politics of the self-conscious and formal kind. As a result, they have evolved a system in which actual political activity is unessential because the Old Man, in one manifestation or another, is always present behind the scenes, where, in return for power, he must see to it that everything runs smoothly. But this point is so complicated and important that I will reserve it for another chapter, where it can be gone into more fully.

What, then, are the common features of all these Japanese fears? First and foremost, they are all uncontrollable, impartial, and transient. The earthquake strikes without regard to race or nationality or social class, and then it is gone. The fire rages for a while but must eventually go out. Thunder, lightning, and typhoons cause immense damage, but when they are over, it is still possible for the survivors to go on. And even the Old Man, sudden and terrible in his wrath, calms down sooner or later; his power is inescapable, but the day comes when it passes into the hands of others.

The nature of things that are feared obviously conditions human reactions to them; the unpredictable and transient disasters feared in Japan have to a large extent determined the way the Japanese think about all dangerous or potentially dangerous situations. For them, persevering means pulling in one's head till the storm is over and then recovering as quickly as possible. An old saying embodies this attitude: Before the smoke has blown away from a burned-down house, the rebuilding hammer can be heard. General MacArthur's occupation of Japan could be regarded as but another natural disaster: in time its effects too would pass. The rages of former prime minister Shigeru Yoshida, an Old Man in the fullest sense, were regarded by the newspapers as misfortunes to be tolerated until they passed, as everyone knew they would. And in recent years, Japan's large share of student violence has often been treated by the local press as nothing but another storm that must be waited out.

But none of this has anything in common with misfortune and disaster as Jews understand these words. For them perseverance is not a matter of a storm of a few hours or days or even weeks but a patient willingness to bear a heavy burden of persecution over many centuries and, even when conditions are good, to know that things must surely get worse soon. Since silent, extended endurance is possible for a whole people but difficult or impossible for the individual, the Jews usually try to do something about distressing predicaments. If it is necessary, they pay for security, become Marranos, or pursue whatever course is necessary to make the situation tolerable.

The act of taking out an insurance policy implies doing something about possible future misfortune. Of course, insurance can assume many forms. The French farmer burying his gold napoleons under the floor is taking out a kind of insurance, just as Mr. Suzuki's elderly Jewish friends were insuring themselves against possible danger by paying high hotel bills. On a larger scale, especially in this age of deterrent strategy, powerful military organizations constitute a kind of insurance against aggression from without. The Japanese, however, totally misunderstand this basic meaning of insurance for the simple reason that they recognize as possible sources of disaster only those forces of nature and society against which no human means can protect them. Consequently, though they are great savers, they put their money away for a bright day, not a dark one. That is, they intend to use their savings for a home, a new car, or their children's education, not as protection against hardship. For these reasons life-insurance salesmen in Japan have always had to press the line that insurance is a kind of savings plan, when in fact it is nothing of the sort.

Jews, on the other hand, believe that a human being not only can but must do something to help himself in time of trouble. Hence they are thoroughly trained in the idea of insurance, of both formal and informal kinds. A number of years ago I heard of a clash between the Japanese and

Jewish ideas about informal insurance that is pertinent here. A young Japanese woman told me that she had heard most unpleasant things about the Jews. When I asked what she meant, she told me the following story.

While visiting in the United States she had overheard an elderly Jew telling a friend that he made it a rule never to reveal to any single member of his family the full extent of his savings, checking accounts, insurance policies, and other provisions for the future. This shocked the Japanese lady; she was appalled at the idea of concealing such information from family members. To her it smacked of the basest stinginess. As she told me: "If all Jews are like that, they deserve the hard things said about them."

But there are a number of considerations the Japanese lady failed to take into account. First, the elderly Jew of her story probably represents a philosophy that no longer prevails among the majority of American Jews. Secondly, his was a way of thinking born of the old and valid insurance principle of dispersal and hiding of resources against time of trouble; that is, as long as no one in the family knows how well off they are as a group, it is impossible for anyone to divulge secrets that might be damaging in case of danger. In the Middle Ages, Jews who endured repeated pillagings of their ghettos learned well that the first step to true insurance is ignorance of the affairs of others and concealment of one's own affairs. To prevent their being discovered and appropriated, family funds were hidden in different places, and their whereabouts were never disclosed in full. When the pillage was over, however, each family would produce its gold and do what it could to help less fortunate neighbors. This Jewish attitude does not indicate a lack of faith in human nature, but rather a wholesome sense of the value of being wary.

The Japanese, on the other hand, are unable to accept this view of human nature. For one thing they have a great faith in humanity, a trait I shall later consider at length. And for another, they cannot imagine making provision to insure themselves against calamity.

At the opening of this chapter I said that attitudes toward security influence the deepest parts of the human heart. In the case of the Japanese, taking security for granted has bred a feeling of blanket trust in mankind that manifests itself in a deep aversion for keeping secrets. The average Japanese cannot rest until he has said whatever is on his mind, whereas the Jew has been conditioned by long centuries of persecution and betrayal to be more guarded. Of course Jews believe in people too; when their instinct tells them to, they can trust others implicitly. But they also know that trusting does not necessarily justify telling everything to everyone. Indeed, to their way of thinking, telling too much can both invite danger and also impose irksome burdens on the listener. The Japanese do not see this; from their viewpoint, keeping secrets falls in the category of such useless security measures as city walls, insurance, or their own Self-Defense Forces.

This feeling of the Japanese is easy to understand in light of the safety they have always enjoyed. In the England of Dickens's time, any woman of class who attempted to travel alone from London to Dover would have been thought insane. Prosper Mérimée makes it clear that the Paris-Marseilles trip in the France of Napoleon III was equally perilous for the unescorted woman. But in these same times it was by no means uncommon for a lone woman to travel on the Tokaido highway linking Edo and Kyoto. Even today Tokyo is known as the safest large city in the world. True, the countries of the Communist bloc also have low crime rates, but there is always the danger of severe punishment for unorthodox thinking. In the so-called free nations of the West one may think as one chooses, but few major Western urban centers can adequately protect their citizens from rape, murder, and theft. By and large, it is only the Japanese who know neither ideological restraint nor a high crime rate. They are blessed indeed, but the blessing is not an unmixed one.

As the Japanese themselves say, too much of a good thing is as bad as too little. Excessive safety and security have turned the Japanese into a cloistered people who panic when faced with crises of even minor severity. For example, when something goes seriously wrong in a government ministry—and when the scandal becomes public knowledge—the reaction almost always follows the same traditional pattern. It is not necessarily the wrongdoers who are punished. Nor do their superiors show a sense of responsibility by trying to iron out the difficulty. Instead it is the man at the top who says something equivalent to "It's all my fault" and resigns.

Perhaps the classic and most distressing example of the Japanese tendency to take more drastic steps than the situation seems to call for is the relatively large number of young people who commit suicide when they fail college-entrance examinations. A similar way out is sometimes taken by an entire family that finds itself in financial straits. And in the final stages of the Pacific War, when any informed person could have known that things were hopeless for Japan, the militarists ran true to form by urging the entire civilian population to fight the Yankee invaders to the last drop of blood and thus find honor in death. (Fortunately, the Japanese were able to ignore this urging for a number of reasons: their basic pragmatism, the fact that others in authority were urging patience, and the ability to view this new disaster as simply another kind of storm that must be ridden out.)

Could the Jews have survived as a people if they had resorted to such dramatic methods? Of course not. Tempered in the furnace of long ages of insecurity and danger, they firmly believe that a practical plan can and must be devised to meet every situation. Instead of falling into a funk and throwing up their hands in despair when the going gets rough, they turn their minds to finding some way to alleviate the trouble. They do this in much the same way as someone might invent a badly needed new machine or tool: after weeding out unworkable ideas from a number of proposals, they settle on a plan and then work hard and single-mindedly to make it succeed. The Jewish love of disputation is famous. Levi Eshkol, the late prime minister of Israel, said that when three Zionists get together they become the makings of five political parties. This may well be true, but it is this very question-and-answer, trial-and-error attitude that saves the Jews from the sort of excessive self-assurance that can so early turn to black despair in the face of difficulty. To the Jew it is perfectly obvious that a good plan of action can result only from a critical examination of a number of possibilities. Therefore he does not hesitate to challenge whatever suggestions are made, even by his wisest leaders, nor does he become suicidal when his own suggestions are criticized or even rejected.

Desperate actions are not the Jewish way; despair would have done no good at Auschwitz.

Perhaps not all Japanese are incapable of coping with the unexpected. An example comes to mind taken from one of the numerous advice-to-the-reader columns found in Japanese newspapers. Some of these columns deal with "life," others with problems peculiar to women or with health; and usually the advice given in answer to questions sent in by readers is at complete variance with what I would expect a Jewish counselor to say under the same circumstances. But once, in a column written by an expert on inventions and research problems, a letter was published that had come not from a would-be inventor but from a woman with an emotional problem. Even though the letter was outside his usual field, the columnist nevertheless decided to answer it. He wrote: "Devise thirty possible solutions to your problem without worrying as to whether they are wise or foolish. I will then select for you the best solution out of the thirty." For a long time he received no answer, but one day a card of thanks arrived saying the problem had been satisfactorily solved by following his suggestion. In this instance, then, the columnist and ultimately his questioner too had followed the Jewish way: improvisation, selection from a number of possibilities, and implementation of a chosen plan.

This is not, however, the usual Japanese approach to a problem. Knowing that desperate acts do not insure continued existence, guarantee security, or satisfy human wants, the Jew has learned to survive by examining the difficulty at hand and devising a way out of it. The Japanese, on the other hand, tends to want to cut through a Gordian knot with one dramatic, and often tragic, stroke when, with only a little application and adaptation, it might have been unraveled to the satisfaction of all concerned. For example, it is not unknown for a Japanese to kill himself because he owes a relatively trifling amount of money. A Jew in similar circumstances would beg and borrow a little here and a little there until he had made up the needed sum, which he could then pay back when times improved. Two thousand years of intimate experience with insecurity, persecution, and misfortune have taught the Jews this valuable lesson. Too much peace and security—and too abundant a supply of water—have hidden these truths from the Japanese.

2. *Animals Sacred and Profane*

A FEW YEARS AGO BRITISH NEWSPA-
pers carried a series of sensational articles on purported
Japanese cruelty to dogs. The texts, but lightly substanti-
ated, were illustrated with photographs of a most unlikely
sort. For instance, men in kimono were shown beating
cowering dogs supposedly kept on chains in conditions of
loathsome filth. While it is not my purpose here to dis-
prove the assertions made in the articles, I think that in
passing it should be noted that the kimono has not been
used for nearly a century in the kind of work performed
in kennels. Occasionally journalistic license produces its
own fancies. However that may be, the Japanese reaction to
the series was a complicated one. One Tokyo daily carried
an article by a pro-Western writer who endorsed the
British claims and explained to his readers that the British
are especially kind to all animals. Another writer, taking

27

quite the opposite line, berated the British for advocating love and care for beasts even though "bloody beef" was a staple in their diets. Still another writer dismissed the entire British view as nothing more than jealousy over Japan's rapid economic progress. Most Japanese, however, were sincerely puzzled to find themselves attacked as abusers of animals, and I think they had every right to this reaction. Fanatical animal lovers and haters exist in both the East and the West, but they are a minority. The average Japanese is not an animal hater, nor is he bent on mistreating animals; rather, his relation to animals is quite different from a Westerner's, and in this difference one discerns aspects of a life view that goes deeper than such superficial manifestations as how one trains and cares for animals.

The human mind tends to treat with special reverence, even to deify, those things on which life depends. Had the journalist mentioned above truly wanted his readers to understand the nature of the Western attitude toward domestic animals he would not have treated as contradictory the British advocation of protection for beasts coupled with a fondness for beef. He would instead have said something to this effect: "The British consider animals worthy of special protection *because* animal flesh is an important part of their diet." The Japanese manifest a similar, apparently contradictory, attitude toward rice. They cut, thresh, and eat it, yet they regard it with the greatest reverence. Though today, with the importation of a wide variety of foodstuffs, the Japanese no longer rely as heavily on rice as they once did, in the distant past it was so important that not a single grain was allowed to go to waste; even the few bits remaining in bowls after meals were carefully saved, stored in jugs, and used later to make glue.

There was a saying to the effect that Kannon, the goddess of mercy, dwelt in every grain of rice. The great seventeenth-century scholar and daimyo of Mito, Tokugawa Mitsukuni, was once roundly scolded by a peasant woman for having dared to sit down on a bale of rice. As the sustainer of life, rice was holy, but no compunctions were felt at cutting the living plant, drying it, and threshing it. In short, as the Westerner can kill and eat the animals on which he lavishes great care, so the Japanese can cut and beat the rice plant, which they consider holy.

To the ancient Jews, sheep were as vital to life as rice to the Japanese of times past because a strong and complex relation exists between nomadic groups and their animals. The sheep gave milk for drinking and for cheese-making; sheep flesh, internal organs, and marrow were eaten; wool was used for clothing and tents; sheep skin was converted into rope, nets, musical instruments, and parchment for scrolls. In the light of the animal's extreme importance to the Jews, it is scarcely surprising that they regarded the lamb as holy. Before World War II, I witnessed in Japan a ceremony conducted by Buddhist mountain priests. In a large bowl-like container with a pedestal, freshly cooked rice was heaped. According to the explanation given me at the time, the steam rising from the rice was being wafted to the eight million gods. I found this especially provocative because of the similarity between this idea and one represented by an ancient Jewish sacrifice. On top of a stone altar, the Jews of old laid a high pile of firewood. On this they placed, then killed, a lamb. Setting fire to the wood, they roasted the lamb and thus sent the fragrant smoke billowing to heaven. In one case the offering is steam from rice, in the other smoke from a burning lamb; but the idea is the same. In this symbolic sense the rice and the lamb become identical.

During the course of their history, the Jews shifted from pure nomadism to a combination of agriculture and live-stock breeding, but they did not abandon this sacrificial rite because they continued to raise sheep in conjunction with farming and because they often came into contact with other nomadic peoples. Gradually, then, "lamb" came to have a special meaning. It is by no means odd that many religious expressions include this word; the Lamb of God in the New Testament, only one example of this usage, in-dicates the sacrificial origin of the image, since this Lamb gives his life so that others may be saved. Most Eurasian peoples have either been, or at one time or another have come in contact with, nomadic sheep breeders. Agricul-tural communities have been conquered by nomads, many of whose customs and ways of life they then adopted. The Japanese, however, are extremely unusual in that they have had little or no prolonged contact with nomads and have never had a society based primarily upon livestock breeding. Talents that other peoples have put into animal husbandry went in Japan into the raising of silkworms. Years ago almost any farmhouse would have had its special loft that had been converted into a silkworm ranch, since the income from selling raw silk was greater than that produced by several acres of riceland. To a Westerner, the white, grub-like silkworms crawling in their fodder are vaguely repel-lent, but to their owners they were once important enough to merit having the honorific prefix (o) attached to the word for silkworm. (Japan now imports raw silk, but at one time those farmers who depended upon sericulture for part of their livelihood were severely affected by changes in the demand for the commodity in the United States. "Everyone paid closest attention to U.S. Steel stock. [Its] shares, being a speculative commodity, were subject to violent fluctuations in price, and therefore proved to be the most accurate barometer of American business. Even today, in the old silkworm belt in Nagano Prefecture, old men remember how they alternated between pleasure and despair as they followed Wall Street news while sitting around the hearths of their old thatched farmhouses on snowy nights."*) One wonders if these sericulturists would find it odd if animal breeders spoke of the "honorable" cow or the "honorable" sheep.

Here the voice of dissent says: "But the Japanese do raise domestic animals." Yes, the warriors of old kept horses, and the farmers cows, but never on a large scale. Furthermore, there was never any intimate relation between human beings and animals, which were considered only tools. A late feudal-period samurai, Sano Genzaemon, once said: "A lance, though it is rusty; and a horse, though it is lean." In other words, the horse is a kind of living weapon. To the farmer the ox or cow supplied power for rice cultivation; it was therefore a convenient though not indispensable tool. The notion of eating the flesh of these animals repelled the Japanese of the distant past. Animal flesh is bloody; consequently it is, in a ritual sense, impure. The traditional Japanese diet—rice, fish, vegetables—generally excludes unclean, or bloody, things. The supposed origin of the now famous Japanese dish sukiyaki illustrates this point. It is said that when forced by necessity to eat beef from time to time, the Japanese cooked it in spades

* Quoted in *The Pacific Rivals,* by the staff of the Asahi newspaper (Weatherhill/ Asahi, New York and Tokyo, 1972).

(suki) to avoid contaminating their ordinary cooking utensils with bloody flesh. The old Japanese viewpoint contrasts with that of Indians, who will not eat the flesh of cows because they consider the animals sacred. The Japanese would not eat it because to them the flesh of four-legged creatures was impure.

Since they thought domestic animals unclean, the Japanese quite consistently regarded the work of slaughtering a task for subhuman outcastes, the Eta. Nomads, on the other hand, believing that raising domestic animals is a religious, even holy, duty, thought butchering a very special task to be handled by priests. In fact, it is said that until the reign of King Josiah, who attempted to turn the Israelites again to the Book of God's Law (about 640 B.C.), ordinary people were forbidden to slaughter their own cattle. Before the religious functions of the nation were centered in Jerusalem, thus making the system no longer practicable, cattle owners took their flocks to special local holy places for slaughter, which was always preceded by a formalized religious ceremony. In Japan the harvesting of rice was equally sacred, and even today the emperor, as high priest, performs ceremonial plantings and harvesting of the grain.

Jews of times past (and many other peoples too) were accustomed to sharing their houses with animals; a single building, divided into an elevated area for the human beings and a lower one for the animals, provided shelter for all. Therefore, the fact that Christ was born in a stable (actually a barn for domestic animals and not a horse stable) aroused no shock. The Japanese, on the other hand, think of animals pejoratively as beasts—one of the few curse words in the Japanese language is *chikusho,* or beast. For that reason, they attach special significance to the place of Christ's birth, to their way of thinking the lowliest possible. When the Japanese poet says "fleas, lice, and horse piss at my pillow," in the Japanese mind he evokes certain unusual associations. To the Jew of the time of Christ, surroundings describable in such terms were only natural.

A house I once visited in a remote village in the upper reaches of the Totsu River in Nara Prefecture was laid out in a way that reveals how preposterous the Japanese consider the idea of living under one roof with foul, four-footed creatures. The house was poor but planned in a logical and interesting fashion. In the main building was the kitchen, where water—that free water of which I have already spoken—flowed constantly from a bamboo pipe. It then ran to the bath, housed in a separate building. From there the water flowed on to clean the privy, also in a separate building, then to the animal barn, where it performed a similar service, and finally to a large cesspool, from which the farmer drew fertilizer for use on the adjoining terraced fields. Clearly, in such a domestic arrangement, the notion of living in the same building with animals was not so much as entertained.

By way of résumé, then, the Jews regarded domestic animals as the basis of life to such an extent that the lamb became a symbol of God and the Saviour of the world. Raising animals was a holy duty, and slaughtering them the work of priests. But the very lack of contact with nomadic traditions bred in the Japanese the idea that four-legged animals were generally impure and that people who slaughtered them were outcastes. It is only to be expected that these disparate approaches manifest themselves in differences of philosophy.

As they do not really understand either the nomadic tradition or true animal husbandry, the Japanese cannot comprehend the rationale and behavior patterns associated with slavery, a less savory kind of animal breeding and care. It is striking that slavery, as known in the West and elsewhere, has never existed in Japan. The Japanese do permit young women to be contracted to the service of geisha establishments or houses of prostitution, and they have used the vanquished in military battles as forced labor, but fundamentally they do not regard human beings as pieces of property that can be bought and sold at will. The geisha, the prostitute, even the apprentice to a tradesman, are looked upon as indentured servants rather than as chattels. They have rights, quite often precisely defined legally, based upon the recognition that they are human beings caught in a set of difficult circumstances.

Slaves, on the other hand, are regarded as little more than beasts, and like other beasts, their purchase, breeding, and sale were taken for granted in countries using the slavery system. (Israel, unlike most Eurasian countries, has never countenanced the keeping of slaves, since it is discouraged in the Laws of Moses.) During the days of the Roman Empire, a slave cost about twice the price of an ass, but as is true of all commodities, his value fluctuated according to the law of supply and demand. After the war against the Jews in A.D. 70, the Romans sold so many of their captives in the slave markets of Greece that the price plunged to half that of an ass, a further blow to the pride of the enslaved. Under ordinary circumstances, however, when the market was not glutted, slaves fetched high enough prices that masters treated them with considerable care. The assertion that slaves were cruelly treated has turned out to be exaggerated. Research has shown, in fact, that slaveowners were most solicitous of their property. In the time of Cato the Elder, on a certain festival day each year, slaves assumed places of honor and masters did the serving. Be all of this as it may, slaves were not treated with the kindness a person shows to a fellow human being. Treatment of slaves was patterned on the practices of all nomadic and animal-breeding groups: take care of the beasts, feed them, and after washing up, go to dinner.

In the distant past, slaves were treated as expensive cattle; in more recent centuries they became articles of large-scale international commerce. Ships designed to hold nothing but slaves—as today there are ships for nothing but automobiles—made ceaseless round trips between Africa and the Americas. Upon being unloaded, the human cattle were exhibited on auction blocks to be sold to the highest bidder. Afterward they were carted off to work in the fields and factories of their new masters.

In addition to work power, slaves brought their masters profit by breeding and producing children, who might be kept or sold when they reached a suitable age, depending on the master's needs. Since sales of young slaves brought in ready cash, females were encouraged to become pregnant as often as possible and were treated with much more care and attention than was shown to gravid cows. I do not imply that men like Simon Legree in *Uncle Tom's Cabin* did not exist. I suggest, instead, that such men were exceptional and that the prevailing attitude of earlier times was that fine slaves should not be maltreated.

Societies revering domestic animals must obviously provide for their charges, but some aspects of care, though occasionally essential to the protection of the species, are far from pleasant in practice. For example, when certain animals in a herd or flock become infected with hoof-and-mouth disease, they must be killed, burned, and destroyed to protect the remainder of the animals from contamination. As slave systems prove, humans too are sometimes treated as cattle. What then happens if some strange virus —for example unorthodox thought, or the suspicion of the existence of such thought—runs rampant through the human herd? For the protection of the majority of the animals, the contaminated members must be destroyed, like victims of hoof-and-mouth disease. Auschwitz and the other Nazi concentration camps perfectly illustrate the destroy-the-contaminated principle. Nazi philosophy saw Jews as beasts contaminated with the disease of being Semitic. In order to protect the healthy animals, it was imperative to kill and burn the Jews. Since they were mere beasts, it was only to be expected that their bones be used for fertilizer, their skin for lampshades, their fat for soap. As the ultimate degradation, the exterminators sometimes demanded fees for their services from the families of the slaughtered victims. But this was not pure cruelty; it was the application of the principle of necessity used to deal with infected animals. During World War II, Japanese soldiers were trained to commit acts of barbarity, but the enemy, while he may have been thought of as inferior, was always a human being. For all the excesses it bred, the Japanese militarist viewpoint never fell to the Nazi level of considering a large group of people as subhuman. The Japanese soldier might decapitate a prisoner, but it did not occur to him or to his superiors to construct slaughterhouses in which thousands of persons could be liquidated as if they were infected animals.

Ironically, the seed of the philosophy put into practice at Auschwitz is to be found in all nomadic peoples at some time or another in their histories. This applies even to the Jews. For example, about two thousand years ago, rabbis denounced with hair-raising ferocity the Am-Haaretz, a group of Jews who were so lax in their ways that they failed to meet the standards of rabbinical orthodoxy. One well-known rabbi went so far as to tell his followers that the Am-Haaretz could and should be torn limb from limb on sight. He was asked if it might not be better said that they could be slaughtered with impunity. But he replied that when animals are slaughtered, blessings are in order and no such auspicious circumstances applied to the vile Am-Haaretz. In other words, in the rabbi's eyes they ranked lower than domestic beasts. By this reckoning the Am-Haaretz were intrinsically foul and contaminating, as the Jews themselves were believed to be by the Nazis. There are stories that Germans bathed themselves thoroughly after accidentally coming into close physical contact with Jews, whereas touching animals was thought in no way polluting. I have earlier mentioned the Eta, but their case is somewhat different in that the Japanese did not think of the Eta as intrinsically impure. Their uncleanness derived from their connection with slaughtering bloody, therefore impure, animals. In short, the discrimination felt against the Eta was occupational. Certain Germans, on the other hand, ranked animals as lower than man but higher than Jews. This is a most definitive brand of discrimination.

The British attack on Japanese treatment of household

pets, cited in the opening of this chapter, rather made the Japanese out to be practicing a special form of discrimination, but, as the intervening discussion suggests, the Japanese treat pets in a way justified by their view of domestic animals in general. Westerners tend to adopt animals into their families and, for better or for worse, to pamper them, although conditions are not always quite so idyllic as was implied by the journalists who concocted the series criticizing the care of dogs in Japan. The Japanese, innocent of the nomad experience, believe that human beings and animals must go their separate ways. Animals are not part of the world that is properly human, but as long as they do not invade the human sphere, peaceful coexistence is possible. If some mutual but not demanding relation can be established, well and good. Japanese history does provide a few exceptions to this principle, the most famous being the actions of the fifth Tokugawa shogun, Tsunayoshi (reigned 1680–1709). When told by a Buddhist monk that he lacked a male heir because he had taken life in a previous existence, the shogun issued a whole series of orders for the protection of all living things. Dogs were specially favored, since Tsunayoshi had been born in the Year of the Dog. So foolishly extreme were his measures that one man was executed for merely wounding a dog, and ultimately vast numbers of the favored animals clogged and befouled the streets of Edo to such an extent that suburban kennels had to be built to house them. It is said that at one time 50,000 dogs were kept and fed in these kennels at the taxpayers' expense. Tsunayoshi was dubbed the Dog Shogun, and although there are small-scale dog shoguns in Japan even today, they are few in number.

The kind of coexistence that the Japanese favor with

respect to animals is illustrated by the packs of monkeys that run free on Mount Takasaki, near Beppu on the island of Kyushu. Tourists visit the spot, are amused by the animals, and feed them rice crackers, but no attempt is made to care for the monkeys in any true way. The animals themselves seem to prefer this indifference.

A cat fancier I know has dozens of stray visitors when food is set out for the house cats, but as soon as the food is consumed the strays retire to their own territories, to reappear only when food is once more put out. To a Japanese this is perfectly natural: the animals can and do take care of themselves; man is not their guardian.

Had the Japanese first existed as nomadic pastoralists, had they then developed fixed settlements primarily given over to livestock breeding, their attitudes toward animals would more closely resemble those of Westerners. But in Japan agriculture was the first dominant industry, and rice became sacred, animals profane. Today, this situation has altered, with the Japanese cheerfully consuming beef, veal, lamb, and pork, but something of the earlier antipathy toward four-legged beasts persists in their live-and-let-live view of the animal kingdom. It may seem to outsiders that the Japanese indifference toward animals results in "cruelty," as defined in the West, but it should be noted that what is really at issue is that the Japanese simply do not react toward the care of animals in a Western way. Societies for the prevention of cruelty to animals or enterprising journalists err in judging them by standards not their own.

As heirs to a great agricultural tradition, the Japanese differ in an even more fundamental way from the heirs of nomadic pastoralists. They have grown up with traditions that stress careful and detailed planning to coordinate growing rhythms with the changes of seasons. This is not to say that the working lives of animal raisers are any the less exigent, but there are long periods in the year when tending rather than doing is the rule, since no amount of frantic activity, no amount of rubbing of the ewes' bellies, will increase the size of a flock. In Japan, the patterns of industriousness traceable to a demanding farming schedule have influenced all kinds of modern management systems. Without taking this into account, one must be cautious about criticizing the Japanese as too restless and overly competitive. Their dedication to hard work, like their attitudes toward animals, must be understood in light of their cultural development.

3. The Fangs of Cronos

THE ANCESTRAL LAND FROM WHICH the Jews take many of their customs (and which today is represented by the State of Israel) is a collection in miniature of the major climatic regions of the earth. The Negev is a desert, yet tropical and malarial zones are not far distant. On a day when Jerusalem is experiencing winter hail—or even occasional snow—only twenty-two kilometers away, as the crow flies, air conditioning is necessary to allay the heat of Jericho. Though the banks of the Jordan are a brilliant jungle, there is always snow atop Mount Hermon. Fertile areas, typically Mediterranean, are present, yet across the eastern highlands lies the Dead Sea in a barren rocky land where nothing but the hardiest of insects can survive. The Israel of the advertising brochures offers the tourist the advantage of being able to choose between swimming and skiing in the same season. It does not seem surprising, then, that from the beginnings of the long Diaspora, Jewish groups have been able to live almost anywhere on the globe without any great sense of shock when confronted with new environments.

This ability of the early Jews to adjust to strange settings was not entirely a matter of having behind them a land of tropical, temperate, and frigid zones, of humid and arid regions, of flatlands and mountains, of rivers and lakes, of fertile areas and salt wasteland. Rather, as many people have pointed out, Palestine, though generous to the hard-working farmer, if neglected even for a short time reverts almost at once to nonarable soil on which sheep raising is the only possible means of making a livelihood. The soil is rich in potassium but water is scarce. Preventing the spring and autumn rains from flowing away unused requires constant attention to soil conservation. As is said in the Mishnah: "He who will not work shall not eat." The demands imposed by this trying environment forced the ancient Jews to cultivate industry, to care for details, to develop a sense of planning, and to make quick responses to environmental changes.

Climate and geography have played an important part in developing the Japanese national personality, as well. The Japanese archipelago is another miniature collection of many of the climatic zones of the world. In the south there are subtropical forests not unlike those of Borneo; in the north the cold and snows are of Siberian severity; and in the vicinity of the capital there is—to borrow from Japanese journalists—the "Tokyo Desert," produced by extremely dry spells typical of the Kanto Plain, especially in winter when cold winds blow. But perhaps the most striking feature of the climate of Japan is the almost precise regularity of seasonal change. The Japanese people are extremely sensitive to these changes, which are the frequent topic of literary comment. Sei-Shonagon, a tenth-century court lady who wrote the famous miscellany *The Pillow Book,* said: "The things that only pass one after another are these: boats with hoisted sails, the ages of man, and spring, summer, autumn, and winter." Because the seasons change rapidly, the Japanese people are forced to alter their living patterns every three months to conform to climatic shifts. This is why I sometimes refer to the Japanese as a ninety-day people. Their lives involve a formidable amount of adaptability and effort because of frequent seasonal changes. As a result, the Japanese tend to seem restless and impatient, as I can illustrate by a very homely comparison. Both the Japanese and the Arabs use tobacco, but the contrasting ways they smoke underscore a fundamental difference in the outlooks of the two peoples. Arabs, leaving everything in the hands of Allah, relax and chat as they enjoy a leisurely hookah. The Japanese, however, cannot spare that much time. Though today it has been supplanted by cigarettes, the traditional Japanese pipe is a long-handled affair with a bowl no larger than a chickpea. Into this the busy Japanese of the past packed a small amount of tobacco. After lighting it from the coals of a charcoal brazier, he took a few hasty puffs, which soon exhausted the supply of tobacco in the pipe. Then, tapping out the ash, he went quickly about his work.

The exigencies of time keep the Japanese constantly active, for as soon as the rainy season has passed the typhoons are certain to come: there is not a minute to waste. A Jewish sage once said that laziness will cause the roof to fall and sloth will make the house leak. The urgency im-

plied by this statement is aptly applied to the Japanese because, in the light of the schedule imposed on them by
nature, if they are indolent they cannot survive.

As the lack of water in Israel makes certain demands on
the people, so natural phenomena and climatic conditions
to a certain extent dictate the actions of peoples everywhere, and the ways in which human groups react and
adapt to these conditions are highly informative. In Japan,
seasonal change has long played an important part in daily
life. Although the English in general do not require summer clothes, since it rarely gets hot in England, the people
living in steamy Singapore have no need of woolens and
winter coats. By contrast, the Japanese need both overcoats
and short-sleeved summer shirts, heating and air conditioning. In the winter the nation is arid, in the spring and
summer humid, and in the autumn typhoons rage over
large parts of the islands. To all of these circumstances the
Japanese have conformed in most effective ways. For example the architectural style *(shinden-zukuri)* of the mansions of the ancient aristocracy and the so-called twelve-
layered costume *(juni-hitoe)* of high-bred ladies of those
times are interesting cases in point. These mansions, designed on an open plan consisting of a main building and
several outbuildings connected by means of covered cor-
ridors, were intended to provide maximum ventilation and
coolness in sultry Japanese summers. Sometimes a small
stream flowing under parts of the house served as primitive
air conditioning. With the approach of winter, however,
the spacious, open buildings became windy and cold.
Since there was no effective heating, elegant ladies of the
time kept warm by putting on more layers of clothing.
The ultimate in warmth—and in elegance—was the twelve-

layered costume. In short, open houses and multiple-layer garments were ways in which the Japanese conformed to their changing climate.

As time passes and people find newer methods of coping with their circumstances, old ways come to seem archaic and inconvenient. No one today would build a house in the shinden style, and the twelve-layered costume would impede active modern living. But the attitudes prompting these adaptations persist. The Japanese—the ninety-day people—are well trained in adapting themselves to circumstances. For instance, Western dress is universally worn in Japanese business life, but the same people who wear suits and ties in the office change into the loose-fitting kimono upon returning home because it meets the needs and moods of domestic life. The ability to make such adjustments is basic to the Japanese; it is not, as noted educator, journalist, and advocate of women's rights Hani Motoko says, imitation and an uneconomical double life.

Climate and geography, then, influence life in many ways, but certainly the most vital and far-reaching of their effects is on agriculture. The Arabs in the vicinity of Palestine, after scattering wheat seed on the ground, lead their flocks to pasture. When the proper time comes, they return to harvest the grain, then go about other business. Their climate makes wheat raising incidental. In the Philippines, where three rice crops are possible in one year, the people plant and harvest more or less whenever they like. But the Japanese climate and reliance—in the past at any rate—on rice as a staple food combine to create circumstances demanding a much more strictly prescribed, campaign-style agricultural system.

The following passage from an old work on agriculture

called *The Farmer's Satchel* shows how the Japanese regard the strict schedule they must maintain if they are to produce enough rice to sustain themselves: "It behooves people to observe heaven's time accurately and to look to local geographical conditions. Farmers must never for a single day fail in these things. The acts of plowing and harvesting depend on heaven's time and on the calendar. The calendar is the official concern of the court, which must grant it to the people. The calendar is the most important concern of the emperor, and it is the treasure of the people. The astrologers must make the calender for the coming year and give it to the emperor in the eleventh month. This is called the bestowal of the calendar. It must then be made available to all places as is the custom in both Japan and China. In Japan, recently, priests of the great Ise Shrine come to bestow the calendar on the people of all the provinces. It is a fortunate custom that this land, the country of the gods, receives the calendar from the Ise Shrine. Above all, the farmer in agricultural work must first observe the calendar with great care. One day's delay means one month's evil fortune. One month's negligence means one hundred days of disaster. The applications of this idea are somewhat different according to local climates and to the signs of divination. Though the time of heaven and of spring, summer, autumn, and winter are the same throughout the provinces of Japan, depending on the location of the region—whether east, west, south, or north—wind, rain, snow, and mist, drought and flood, cold, heat, warmth, and coolness all differ. Moreover, grasses, trees, and other things differ from region to region. Although the cycle of the seasons is the same for the whole country, the blessings or misfortunes it bestows differ for the sixty-six provinces, each of which has its own peculiar conditions. It is therefore necessary to give profound attention to all local conditions in detail. Not a single plant or tree will flourish if planted without consideration of local variations. We speak of differences among houses, but all things are one body in the truth of heaven and earth, and differences occur because of the four directions and the eight positions. Places that are one or two *ri** distant have many dissimilarities. Clearly, then, places forty ri apart are not the same in land or climate. One must study with people who know the geography of the land well."

This passage brings out two very important points: the absolute necessity of adhering to a tight agricultural schedule and the importance of adjusting both that schedule and other agricultural activities to the geographical nature of the locale. The harvest time in Japan is fixed; therefore, every aspect of farming must be back-calculated from that time. "One day's delay means one month's evil fortune." A single day of delay must be made up with a life-and-death frenzy of activity, for even that small lag spells the difference between a one-hundred-percent crop and a zero crop. Inevitably typhoons come in harvest time; consequently, the rice seedlings must be planted in March, transplanted to the paddies during the rainy season, and harvested before the storms can spoil the crop. In the light of this rigid schedule, the Japanese attitude that each task has its appointed time and that no negligence can be permitted is scarcely surprising.

In the Middle Ages eighty-five percent of the population of Japan farmed the land. This means that for at least ten

* One *ri* is about four kilometers.

centuries, the vast bulk of the Japanese people has been subjected to the rigorous training inherent in campaign-style agriculture. As a result, no people on earth is as good at setting dates and, working back from them, establishing second-by-second schedules. In addition, probably no other people is as deeply imbued with the unquestioning belief—also derived from campaign-style agriculture—that effort in itself will produce satisfactory results. This attitude is of course no longer limited to agriculture but extends to all aspects of Japanese life. Some unfavorable and favorable events coming from its application include the attack on Pearl Harbor, the postwar recovery of some of the nation's largest business firms, the Tokyo Olympics in 1964, EXPO '70, and, most recently, the Winter Olympics in Sapporo.

Of course other peoples use plans and schedules in large-scale programs, but none carries them out with the split-second accuracy of the Japanese. For example, the Soviet Union has a planned economy, but in frequent cases the plan does not run according to schedule. Hydroelectric power stations were delayed for years because, though the turbines were ready, the generators were not. To the Japanese such slipshod implementation of a plan is inconceivable. On the other hand, certain peoples find the Japanese you-can-do-anything-if-you-try attitude nothing short of mad. The nomadic shepherd knows that rubbing a sheep's belly or busily attempting to breed animals that are not in heat will do nothing to increase his flock. From his standpoint Japanese adherence to a rigid timetable is utterly incomprehensible and almost lunatic. Since Eurasians combine the nomadic and agriculturalist ways of life, their approaches to planning differ from those of the Japanese.

Especially, they consider the Japanese willingness to work even without proper return bewildering. To them the Japanese system of subcontracts—which is much like Japanese tenant rice farming—is unintelligible. Small Japanese companies under subcontracts work hard to accomplish a task, even if the provisions of their contracts are not fulfilled by the main contractor. They realize that given the stiff competition in Japanese business they cannot count on further work from the main contractor unless they demonstrate great industry. Undercapitalized, usually short of reserve funds, the small independents must make sacrifices that seem unjustified to the Western world, where criticism of the Japanese failure or inability to reduce the number of marginal producers in an otherwise highly sophisticated economy is often voiced. To Westerners, especially Eurasians, the Japanese system seems a waste of time and energy. Yet the Japanese, willing to work hard and to ignore the niceties of contractual arrangements, have made such remarkable progress that their critics are disarmed. The heirs of a nomadic tradition cannot hope to imitate the Japanese way of doing things; they lack the long centuries of training in industriousness—blind or enlightened as it may be—that the Japanese have experienced.

Campaign-style agriculture has given the Japanese one more distinguishing trait: a sense of the unity of all the people of the nation. As I said, in the Middle Ages eighty-five percent of the population farmed the land. This meant that at any given period of the year, almost everyone was doing the same kind of work. When the season came to transplant the rice seedlings into the paddies, the entire farming population was engaged in that activity. The exigencies of campaign-style agriculture forbade a going-my-own-way attitude. Since hunger and destitution were the certain outcome of such independence, anyone who insisted on adopting it inevitably became a burden on his neighbors. A Japanese farmer I know well once said: "I am neither an industrious nor a conscientious farmer; I am merely a neighbor farmer." Obviously he was being modest, but what he meant by a "neighbor farmer" is this: when his neighbor plants seedlings, fertilizes the ground, or harvests the rice, my farmer friend must be doing the same thing. That is, he does what his neighbor does, and every other farmer in Japan does likewise. If the neighbor he selects as a model is a good farmer, he is on the road to success. I am aware that there are people who would criticize this way of doing things as shockingly lacking in initiative, but I cannot agree. First, the act of selecting a good model demonstrates initiative. Second, in order to copy the actions of the neighbor, a farmer must possess a comparable level of skill, which requires considerable initiative to attain. Some people might object that to carry the neighbor-farmer concept to its logical conclusion is to arrive at the stage where one must "keep up with the Joneses," that is, buy a new piano or color television set whenever the neighbors do so. I do not feel that is necessarily true. For instance, the skill with which the Japanese maintained their national character while learning new techniques and ideas from the West after the Meiji Restoration of 1868 indicates that the neighbor-farmer idea need not end in slavish imitation.

Among the most important benefits Japan derived from the neighbor-farmer idea as applied to learning from the West were the surprisingly rapid spread of mandatory education, the rise in the national literacy rate that took place in the Meiji period, and the spread of university education following the end of World War II. The nations of Southeast Asia and the Arab world, on the other hand, vividly show the effects on education of a going-one's-own-way attitude, for in those areas all attempts at compulsory education laws came to nothing. What their neighbors are doing fails to affect these peoples at all. This is certainly not true of the Japanese, as the following story about the mother of Hideyo Noguchi, famous bacteriologist, reveals. In her childhood, her family was too poor to send her to school, but she eavesdropped at classroom windows and learned to write by scratching the characters being taught in the sand with her fingertip. Had this program of self-education been inspired by a love of learning for its own sake, she would have continued studying throughout her life. Since she apparently did not, one wonders if her dedicated attempt was not inspired by the compulsion, inculcated by her culture, to do as all others were doing. Similarly, today the sense of unity with all other Japanese that is fostered by campaign-style agriculture leads some people to lament that their children cannot earn a university degree. The regret arises not from an awareness of the nobility of education but from envy that the neighbors' children are going to college. In a social setting of this kind, true independents are bound to meet one of two fates: society will either reject them or correct them. In the future the fiery young members of radical student groups will probably provide ample evidence of the effects of society's rejection or correction.

One legacy of more than two thousand years of submerging the individual in the group is a scarcity of internationally known Japanese. Even during the revolution and turmoil of the Meiji period, when Japan opened wide her doors to all kinds of Western influences, there was no call for a charismatic Napoleon, Lenin, or Mao Tse-tung to lead the government and the people. The group acted instead. Something very similar was true of postwar economic recovery. Who proposed the recovery plans? Who led them? A former Japanese ambassador once remarked that although everyone knows who De Gaulle, Mao, and Nehru are, aside from some Japanophiles, few Westerners have heard of Shigeru Yoshida. The only post-Meiji prime minister to gain a certain degree of international fame was Hideki Tojo, but now even he is almost forgotten. Nor is this surprising; after all, what kind of dictatorial figure does a man famous as a good husband and father cut? Interestingly, this lack of dramatic authoritarian leaders is reflected in the nature of assassinations in Japan. No one has ever assassinated a political figure with the aim of ridding the nation of a despot because there have been no despots.

The nomad world has never experienced the necessity for a whole people to move together in one line of endeavor. Indeed, anyone desiring to institute such a policy must first of all realize that unless the Arab sands are held tightly in the hand, they slide away in all directions. Able literally to go their own way, owners of flocks of sheep were in the past and are today free to lead their animals over boundless and boundary-less plains of grasslands. The Koran and the sword—that is, religion and power—are the only things that have ever successfully galvanized into unity peoples accustomed to the untrammeled nomadic way of life. Even these two forces required the stimulus of either an enemy or a powerful competitor to unify their followers. The most moderate of the nomads' slogans has been "chase and overtake," and when such mottoes have failed to prevent the peoples from splitting again into their many factions, the threat of a Jewish state has always been a sufficient force to forge the nomads into unity, even if only temporarily. The Japanese have never needed either slogans or exterior stimuli to bind them together, but no other nation on earth can achieve the unity they maintain. Mao Tse-tung is trying to weld all of the people of China into a body moving on a line of uniform action. Put in extreme terms, his attempt amounts to converting the Chinese into something like the Japanese. I do not know whether he will succeed. Certainly without a man of his stature, the task is impossible. But even so, the Chinese—and no other people—can become what the Japanese already are.

On the whole, the Japanese achievements in devising ways to master the demanding schedule imposed on them by environment are admirable, but they have a less attractive side. The cruelly exacting schedule imposed by campaign-style rice production magnifies the significance of time in all Japanese activities, both work and leisure. It is as if, year in and year out, the Japanese are constantly running in front of the gleaming fangs of that ancient symbol of time, Cronos, who had the grisly habit of devouring his own children. Completely absorbed in maintaining their to-the-second schedules, the Japanese dash madly through the days and months. Everything is a dream, but in the evening years of life, when they finally pause to reflect on the past, Japanese fall victim to a sickening sense of transience and vanity. Having spent all of their lives running at breakneck pace to stay in front of the jaws of time, in the final analysis they see life as no more than a long parade of disconnected events. When faced with the apparent meaninglessness of their own cycle, they often feel that the

truly enlightened people are those who boldly leap on
Cronos's back and ride along with time instead of rushing
blindly in front of it. A Japanese who worked as a technical
adviser in Arabia for a number of years commented that
while there he had been forced to reevaluate his interpretation of life and time because of the influence of the Arabian
people. This is no doubt the truth, since the nomads are
always riding on the back of time. Their place there, however, has nothing to do with enlightenment. In fact, they
regard as enlightened the occasional nomad who is willing
to race at the tip of Cronos's nose. To their way of thinking,
human beings, animals, grasses, trees, and all things are
born of the earth, to which they must return. The world
of nature is eternal and immobile, and man, astride the
back of time like all other things, must pass in his turn.
Eternity is now, and both a thousand years and a split
second are the same in the time of God. It is because of this
attitude that the nomads have never produced a writer like
Sei-Shonagon, for whom the passing of things is moving and
important.

Their interpretation of the nature of the passage of time
makes the nomads extremely difficult for the Japanese to
understand in terms of daily life. For example, suppose a
Japanese reader comes across a passage in the Scriptures in
which God, or His prophet, commands a man, or a group
of men, to wait for a special event for no more reason than
that "it is written." A Japanese, forever aware of Cronos,
would fail to see the sense of the passage. If he were the one
ordered to wait, he would soon begin to fidget impatiently
and wonder how much longer he must waste his time. But
for the nomad, waiting is just another aspect of riding the
current of time. The following story of the Jews of Yemen

illustrates the nomadic belief that time is an unbroken continuum in which lengths of individual temporal units are insignificant.

A group of Jews who had been living in Yemen for almost two thousand years in virtual isolation from contacts with the outer world heard, almost as if it were written on the wind, that God had kept His promise and that they once again had a homeland in Israel. Some 43,000 people—the entire Yemen Jewish population with a few special exceptions—rose up and started walking to Israel. Men, women, and children crossed mountains and deserts to arrive at Aden, where amazed representatives of the government of the State of Israel arranged for transport planes to carry the multitude to Israel. Government employees were astounded at the nonchalance with which these Jews had left everything, endured great hardships, and finally boarded planes to take them home. It was as if the two thousand years of their isolation had never existed. When asked about their apparent indifference, the Jews from Yemen said: "It is written in the Word of God that we must mount on the wings of eagles and return to the Promised Land."

This now famous airborne mass migration happened in the twentieth century; it is not something quoted from the Bible and thus liable to discredit as legend. Japanese find it difficult to believe that the Yemen Jews would embark on such a great movement after two thousand years. But when I ask them how they would feel if I said that the emigration had taken place after an isolation of only ten or one hundred years, they seem to think this reasonable. The point is that to the nomads, riding along on the current of time, there is no essential difference between two years or two thousand years. But the differences between such temporal periods are essential indeed if one is dashing in front of the fangs of Cronos.

Japanese Christians claim to understand the theory that all time is one, but even they cannot avoid fidgeting as they wait, because they are always conscious of the monster Cronos chasing at their heels. For this reason I do not believe that there are any true Christians in Japan. One of the basic tenets of Christianity is the Second Coming of Christ. No one knows when this will be; therefore, Christians have no choice but to wait for it. If the Japanese must wait for the millennium in the same frantic and fidgety way that they wait for everything else, they will all perish of nervous breakdowns. But I shall go into this topic more thoroughly when I speak of Nihonism, the religion that I believe is the national faith of Japan.

4. Villa People, Highway People

COMPARING JAPAN AND PALESTINE always makes me feel that God has been unjust in the distribution of his blessings. A gardenlike villa just off the Eurasian land mass, Japan has provided its people with a fortunate environment in which hardships are few. But the geographical situation of Palestine has made of the Jews waifs hurled onto the great highway linking Eurasia and Africa. One of the greatest advantages isolation has given the Japanese is that their islands have not been constantly turned into battlefields. Some Japanese might object that their history is full of warfare, but I would consider such an objection an indication of a lack of knowledge about the nature of true warfare and of a failure to appreciate the blessedness of the Japanese situation. To substantiate my argument, let me make a few comparisons between the kinds of battles that have taken place in Japan and in the Middle East.

Two of the most important wars in all Japanese history were the Hogen Insurrection (1156) and the Heiji War (1159–60). In the former, the foundations were laid for the erection of a feudal state, and in the latter, the Genji clan triumphed over the Heike clan and thus opened the road for themselves to build that state in actuality. But neither of these was a true war of the cataclysmic kind known in the West. As the very name of the first suggests, it, and the latter as well, were coups d'état of the kind that occur so frequently today in Eurasia, Africa, and South America that they scarcely seem to deserve detailed historical record. But in passing I should like to mention one interesting outcome of these struggles: they brought about the reinstitution of the death penalty in Japan, where for two centuries capital punishment had been abolished. Two hundred years without the death penalty might well be the dream of any nation.

It is true that in the late fifteenth and early sixteenth centuries Japan experienced a period known by the awe-inspiring title—borrowed from China—of *Sengoku Jidai,* or the Period of the Country at War. In fact, however, the title conveys more grandeur than the events deserve, for the contesting factions rarely represented anything larger than a province, and the actual fighting was tame when set against the bloody slaughters to which the Middle East and Europe had been accustomed for centuries. The greatest battle in Japanese history, Sekigahara (1600), which was over in half a day, resembled a tournament of knights more than a war. At the opening of the encounter each side indulged in the courtly ceremony of reading scrolls of family lineages; local farmers prepared lunches and made excursions to watch the fighting. Even the great sieges of Osaka Castle, called the Summer and Winter Campaigns (1614–15), fail to amaze with either their length or their ferocity. Although Osaka Castle was the largest fortress in Asia at the time, the sieges themselves make a poor showing in comparison with Nebuchadnezzar's siege of Tyre.

In sharp contrast to the relative mildness of Japanese internal war, turbulence and bloodshed have plagued the peoples of the Middle East for three thousand years. Each autumn, when the farmers have harvested their produce, the nomads set out to do their own reaping, which consists in attacking the farmers, seizing the fruits of their year's work and whatever cattle they own, killing resisters and those who refuse to move, and carrying off less recalcitrant victims into slavery. After setting fire to whatever they cannot haul away, the nomads vanish into the desert without a trace. Similarities between accounts of plundering nomads in the tales of Gideon and the impressions recorded by a traveler in Palestine in 1936 bear witness to the antiquity and persistence of this cruel custom. In robbing the tillers of the land, nomads feel no pangs of conscience. Just as the farmers rejoice over a good crop, so the raiders are glad when their pillaging excursions are successful. When the late King ibn-Saud of Arabia ascended the throne in 1932, he realized that unless he put a stop to these raids agriculture would never progress and the nomads would never settle down. Finding no moderate way to bring order to his subjects, he commanded that everyone—to the last child—who participated in further raids must be shot. To be sure, his step was extreme, but in the light of the circumstances, one must not criticize it without serious thought: in all likelihood he had no other way out of the dilemma. Visitors to Israel often see memorial markers to Jews slaughtered in the early days of this century by nomad raids on established settlements. But Jews are not the only victims of such attacks. If similar memorials were to be erected for all of the Arab fellahin slaughtered by nomadic tribes, Palestine would become a forest of cenotaphs.

To prove that the nature of internal strife in Japan, even during the age of the Country at War, differs sharply from that in the Middle East I need not add more concrete examples. Reference to the letters of the Jesuit missionaries living in Japan during the fifteenth and sixteenth centuries should make my point clear. These men, who had either visited or heard about most of the Orient and the Middle East of their age, were unusually knowledgeable. According to their correspondence, Japan was one of the most peaceful and secure nations of the world of their time.

Now, leaving the subject of internal war, let us turn to the topic of invasions by aggressors from without. Here the Japanese have had one experience that until World War II they considered the gravest crisis the nation ever faced: the invasions by Mongols in 1274 and again in 1281. But, in comparison with invasions as known in Eurasia, just how serious were the Mongol incursions? Not very, as the events themselves show. Since the only areas of Japan the Mongols managed to invest were the islands Iki and Tsushima and part of Hakata in northern Kyushu, total occupation of the nation was patently impossible even if the divine wind (kamikaze) of a typhoon had not come to the rescue by destroying many of the Mongols and their fleet. After taking their small corner of northern Kyushu, the Mongols had no serious chance of making their way to Kyoto, for the way there led through the Inland Sea, in those days swarming with pirates of the most desperate sort. Had they decided on the mountain instead of the water route, they would have been open to constant attacks from land and sea and would therefore have been unable to secure their supply lines. In bogs, mountains, rice paddies, and rivers guerrilla bands would have blocked them in all directions. But most frustrating of all, allowing the Mongols more good luck than common sense suggests they could have had and supposing that by some miracle they had managed to take Kyoto, the prize would have been empty, for that city was not then the capital of the nation. The true seat of the government was at Kamakura, located at a great distance from Kyoto behind a range of forbidding mountains. Only a fool would have attempted to attack it, especially since merely securing the rear was an impossible task. Even had the Mongols launched so mad a plan, bands of Japanese samurai and armed farmers would have cut them down murderously. When examined with a dispassionate and critical eye, the supposedly horrendous invasions of the Mongols boil down to this: the enemy pushed its way into Japan, temporarily occupied a small region of one of the major islands, but from the very beginning lacked sufficient armed power, equipment, and supply capabilities to make full-scale occupation of the nation feasible.

Campaigns of this kind are yearly occurrences in Eurasia; and Palestine, the land bridge, has for centuries been the scene of more gruesome battling. Great armies have attacked from the regions of the Tigris, Euphrates, and Nile rivers. The peoples of the sea have pressed inland or have followed the Palestine coast in their sorties into Egypt.

Giving detailed accounts of all of this fighting is unnecessary, since they are well known, but even these few examples amply illustrate the difference between the traditional peace of Japan and the mayhem that has beset the Middle East for ages. Palestine's history has indeed been tempestuous, but I do not imply that the Jews are the only people to have experienced such horrors as captivity and genocide. To cite only one example, as Dawson's history of the Mongols reveals, Genghis Khan and his warriors committed acts of hair-raising barbarism and violence throughout Eurasia.

Brought up in a parklike land of peace, the Japanese knew very little of the true nature of war, and their ignorance in this connection has led them into strange paths. For instance, after the nineteenth-century opening of the nation to Western influences, the Japanese decided to try their skill at Western warfare. Their striking successes in the Sino-Japanese War of 1894–95 and the Russo-Japanese War of 1904–5 seem to have gone to their heads to the extent that they began to believe in their own invincibility. Against this background, the attitudes and behavior of the militarists in the years preceding World War II become somewhat easier to understand. But even in the defeat suffered in that great war, the Japanese never saw their homeland turned into a battlefield. I suspect that they never will have this experience, and the very lack of such knowledge causes them to assume an attitude toward peace that I find incorrigible. When they loudly insist that all nations must preserve the kind of peace that they have almost always known, they remind me of Marie Antoinette's suggesting that the starving poor eat cake instead of bread. On the other hand, the Japanese are not—as was once alleged —a nation of mental twelve-year-olds. Raised in a peaceful country, they are talented; but their ignorance of the world outside their islands often causes them to become tense in the face of problems they do not understand. They are well-bred people who stand in amazement before a wider world where impudence often passes as virtue. Neither inefficient nor fatuously good-natured, they possess special abilities resulting from more than a thousand years of thorough training in campaign-style agriculture. The peculiar nature of their background and abilities makes it impossible to judge them on the basis of criteria suitable to the evaluation of other peoples. Therefore, the rationale that an understanding of B naturally follows from an understanding of A must be discarded in this case.

Blessed by never having known the bitterness of plunder, carnage, and massacre on their own shores, the Japanese have almost never known the sorrow of losing their homeland. There is, however, an exception to this generalization, for if the secret Christians of the seventeenth century were the only Japanese ever to have lived in an inner ghetto, the only Japanese ever to be forced from their native land were a group of exiles best represented by the sad Oharu of Jagatara.

When I was younger there was a Japanese popular ballad about Oharu, and it may have been the lyrics of that song that prompted me to look up the deeply moving series of letters called the *Jagatara-bumi* (Letters from Jagatara). When the Tokugawa shogunate decided to embark on a policy of isolation in the first half of the seventeenth century, the government issued a number of decrees dealing with the exclusion of foreigners and with the exile to Jagatara—an old Japanese pronunciation of modern Djakarta—of the children and grandchildren of foreigners by

Japanese mothers. One of these exiles was Oharu, a woman who wrote what are, in fact, love letters to her lost homeland. Her opening line "Though it is October, here there are still fireflies" sounds like something one might write to a lover who is far away, but Oharu is lamenting the loss of her country, the land that had been like a mother to her. She ends another letter in this way: "Even to this day, I have never worn the clothes of this land. Though exiled here, how is it possible for me to become one of these people? Ah, beloved Japan, how I long to go home, how I want to see you, to see you, to see you!" I imagine that had it been possible she would have smuggled herself on a ship to return to Japan though she knew she would be put to death if caught. Oharu later married a Chinese, but she continued to send letters to Japan until her death at the age of seventy-six. Her child too wrote letters to Japan until ordered by the government to stop. At this point, the child fades into oblivion. Like Oharu, there have been Jews who have returned to Palestine though knowing that they ran the risk of execution for their act. The profound love Oharu felt for her homeland, a devotion handed on to a child born in a foreign land, is very much like the Jewish devotion to Zion and the grief the Jews felt over its loss. But, whereas in Japan virtually no one has been forced to make this sacrifice, for the Jews the Diaspora was the general state of affairs for centuries.

The good fortune of a peaceful homeland from which there is no danger of expulsion is a fine thing. But taking the blessed state for granted leads to trouble. For instance the young person raised in the villa sometimes does and says things that show he is a spoiled child after all. I should like to give a few examples of my meaning.

Japanese writers frequently express themselves on both trivial and important questions with a complacency and haste that fail to take the background of the issue into consideration. In addition, they often assume the tone that their pronouncement is absolutely true and that there is no latitude for discussion. For example, an article that appeared in the *Asahi Shimbun,* one of the largest and most prestigious newspapers in the nation, claimed that the Self-Defense Forces should not use traditional artillery salutes to welcome visiting athletes to the 1964 Olympics because they were entirely out of keeping with the peaceful nature of the games. Clearly, the writer had not bothered to investigate either the background or the meaning of the traditional and internationally recognized gun salute. Although a number of explanations of the custom have been advanced, it is generally understood as a proclamation on the part of the host nation that it has voluntarily disarmed and is greeting its guests in peace and friendship. Once old-fashioned cannons were loaded, the only way to unload was to fire them. As a ship entered a port with cannons thrusting from its hatches, no one could tell whether the guns were loaded. But if that ship fired its weapons while still in the offing and if the cannons remained in full view for the remainder of the entry into port, manifestly the ship had voluntarily disarmed. The same thing applied to the cannons of shore emplacements. In short, the firing of the weapons is a symbol of peace and good will. Failure to fire the artillery salute might possibly—though not probably— be taken as indication of warlike intentions. In other words, the silence of the ceremonial guns symbolically says: "I am ready and will shoot when need be." Surely this would not have been a suitable greeting for athletes who visited Japan for the Olympic games. Obviously the journalist who composed the newspaper piece never thought of this. But, in the final analysis, no matter what he had in mind, his words were liable to such an interpretation, and his failure to realize that possibility reveals a laxness of which Japanese are sometimes guilty.

A second example of failure to examine the nature of situations carefully and to trace their possible ramifications before making pronouncements involves abandoning the old-fashioned method of reckoning dates by means of reign periods and of establishing the Western calendar in its place. Once again the *Asahi Shimbun* published an article on the topic, saying that since the rest of the world used the Western calendar the Japanese ought to adopt it exclusively. The important point here is the phrase "the rest of the world." With what a cavalier gesture the Japanese dismiss from membership in the world the Muslims, who have their own calendar, the Hinayana Buddhists, who have theirs, and the Chinese who date from the founding of the Chinese Republic. Oddly enough, even though they are constantly talking about Asia and Asian problems, in this instance the Japanese remove the majority of Asiatic peoples from the roster of world members without so much as a backward glance. But the heart of this problem centers on the term "Western calendar," for it is in fact a misnomer. Dating everything from the birth of Christ, it ought to be called the Christian calendar. This is especially true since the only nations using it are those that either are now or were in the past Christian (including some of the currently Communist nations and the colonies of Christian countries). Of course, I am aware that "Western calendar" is used largely for convenience and is in this respect unexceptionable. But it is not, in fact, as universally convenient as is sometimes thought. For example, what dating system must the emperor of Japan use in writing a friendly letter to the president of the United Arab Republic, the emperor of Iran, or the king of Thailand? One can easily imagine the amusement of the president of the United Arab Republic upon receiving a letter from the Japanese emperor dated 1,972 years after the birth of Jesus Christ.

Compromises may be made for the sake of convenience: the Jews themselves employ the so-called Western calendar with a slight modification, though on most formal occasions they use traditional dating. For example, Israel's declaration of independence is dated 5708, the fifth day of the month of Iyar. Below this, however, is appended May 14, 1948. I have said that the so-called Western calendar is most accurately termed the Christian calendar, but the Jews, while using it, do not recognize its religious significance. For that reason they have abandoned B.C. and A.D. in favor of C.E. for Common Era and B.C.E. for before the Common Era. Finding the Western calendar convenient in international dealings, the Jews use it but they do not give up the traditional dating system. This seems to me the system the Japanese ought to adopt. They will of course have to employ the Western reckoning for convenience, but there is no reason to abandon the older reign-period system. Should the Japanese ever discard reign periods (I cannot believe that they ever will), since the nation is not Christian, it logically would be forced to use the B.C.E. and C.E. designations. This, unfortunately, would put the Japanese in the position of being somewhat ridiculous for copying the Jews.

Though the first of my two examples indicates individuality and independence and the second a tendency to be part of a larger group, at the bottom of both attitudes is a certain spiritual weakness that clearly sets the Japanese apart from the Jews, abandoned, as I have said, in a land that is a highway. Though talented and vigorous, the spoiled Japanese tend to rely on people too much. Today the revolutionary camps have much to say about orphans of the world and particularly of Asia. It is strange to apply the word to the Japanese, but they too seem to be expressing the orphan theory in a slightly unusual way when they maintain unarmed neutrality, which is made possible by the guarantees of the United States, China, and the Soviet Union. They seem to think that the United States is a rich papa and the Soviet Union a devoted mother with an eye out to all kinds of social guarantees. In this analogy, the British ruling party becomes big brother, and all the countries of Asia are younger brothers and sisters. I do not think the analogy is ever advanced seriously; even if it were, it would meet with scorn. Not many years ago, when China was in an especially energetic stage of activity, a certain cultured Japanese said that Japan will be unable to carry on unless it becomes a tributary of China. What he, and all the other spoiled Japanese children, failed to realize is that China would hasten to reject an offer that Japan become her tributary because all sensible nations, well aware that people when offered an inch frequently take a mile, would consider it madness to establish any kind of protectorate over a nation as frighteningly active as Japan. To do so would be to acquire a competitive force that could prove extremely difficult to control.

In politics and in many other fields, Japanese make strange proposals that no one bothers to refute. The articles on the artillery salutes for the Olympics and the project for abandoning traditional reign periods excited no rebuttal. It often happens that similar ill-advised projects are silently stifled. Their advocates only rage all the louder at being squelched; but, though no one says anything decisive against them, they invariably fail to achieve their ends: the Olympics had their artillery salutes, and it is entirely unlikely that the reign periods will ever go out of use. The dog barks, but the caravan moves silently on. To move forward in silence and to establish directions of action without being aware of doing so are inherent aspects of the Japanese character and part of the hidden Japanese political genius. In the next chapter I shall talk about the nature of this genius and shall attempt to discover whether it is based on a clear political philosophy.

5. *Politics Abstract and Pragmatic*

AFTER TITUS DESTROYED THE TEMPLE in A.D. 70 and after the Romans replaced the names Judea and Jerusalem on their maps with the new names Palestina and Aelia Capitolina, autonomous Jewish political activities on a national scale ceased. They were not to be revived until the twentieth century. The development of rabbinical learning and of the institution of the synagogue in the centuries following the Diaspora, however, gave the Jews a focus around which to orient all phases of secular and religious life. As a result, religious ideas became an important aspect of political thought for the Jews. This was not unusual, since most peoples have at one time or another used religion to reinforce the powers of rulers.

Advocates of the separation of the authority of church and state have pointed out the many dangers that exist when nations mix religious and political powers. It seems that such separation is, in fact, indispensable to the successful functioning of the legislative, executive, and judicial structures in most modern democratic states. Dante, in his political writings, insisted that the Holy Roman Emperor should abandon any pretensions to religious authority and that the Pope keep his hands out of politics. Medieval European history, especially during the reign of Boniface VIII, reveals the lack of enthusiasm on the part of both secular and sacred leaders to respond to the poet's advice. But poets and visionaries often go unheeded. Dante did, and so did the Minor Prophet Zechariah, who advised the Jews to make a clear distinction between temporal and spiritual powers. Although his words bore no practical results, his ideas deserve some attention as a rare example in Jewish history of his kind of political thinking.

True to the apocalyptic tradition, Zechariah's writings are generally difficult to understand, but the following passage is clear enough as an expression of his basic beliefs: "And the word of the Lord came to me: 'Take from the exiles Heldai, Tobijah, and Jedaiah, who have arrived from Babylon; and go the same day to the house of Josiah, the son of Zephaniah. Take from them silver and gold, and make a crown, and set it upon the head of Joshua, the son of Jehozadak, the high priest; and say to him, "Thus says the Lord of hosts, 'Behold, the man whose name is the Branch: for he shall grow up in his place, and he shall build the temple of the Lord. It is he who shall build the temple of the Lord, and shall bear royal honor, and shall sit and rule upon his throne. And there shall be a priest by his throne, and peaceful understanding shall be between them both.'" And the crown shall be in the temple of the Lord as a reminder to Heldai, Tobijah, Jedaiah, and Josiah the son of Zephaniah.' " (Zech. 6:9–14)

This means that the man whose name is Branch shall build the temple of Jehovah and shall sit on the throne and rule. At his side shall be a priest, and there shall be peace between the two. Although the man named Branch rules, the high priest accepts the crown of authority in his name, and ultimately it is kept in the Temple. Thus the man named Branch can govern only with the approval of the high priest. As the passage suggests, the two will work together harmoniously without interfering with each other's proper activities. Had such a system been established, Jewish history might have been quite different. But Zechariah went unheeded and his vision ended as only a dream.

The Japanese, on the other hand, made a splendid success of the separation of secular and religious powers. As his descent is traced from Amaterasu, the Sun Goddess, the emperor of Japan has always been associated with divine powers and his functions have been largely limited to the performance of religious ritual. Political and executive powers have been delegated to or assumed by others. This division was given organizational form in the twelfth century when Minamoto Yoritomo established a completely separate military government, or shogunate, in a town called Kamakura, some distance from Kyoto, the seat of the imperial court. From that time until the middle of the nineteenth century, Japan was governed under a dual system that carefully distinguished temporal and spiritual authority. It is true that similar systems have been tried, sometimes with success, by other peoples, but the Japanese version operated smoothly and persisted for many ages because the populace was psychologically conditioned from time immemorial to accept such a system as perfectly natural. Of course, this was not the only secret of the Japanese system's success. Unless real power was concentrated in the hands of the administrative authorities, ambitious emperors and court nobles could not be kept in splendid impotence. By and large, shoguns managed to hold the reins firmly, thereby assuring the perpetuation of the system. When they failed to do so, upheaval followed, terminating in the establishment of a new shogunate. In other words, though the ruling families changed from time to time, the system endured.

Occasional attempts to restore imperial authority at the expense of the shogunate illustrate both the power of the executive rulers and the deep reverence they felt for the emperor as a symbol of the nation and as the fountainhead from which flowed all honors, including the very legitimacy of shogunal rule. For example, in 1221 the clever and audacious cloistered emperor Go-Toba used his prestige and his wits in an attempted overthrow of the Kamakura government, then controlled by the powerful Hojo regent Yoshitoki. In the end, Yoshitoki proved strong enough to exile Go-Toba, but never for a moment did he attempt to detract from the ceremonial preeminence of the imperial rank. When Go-Toba assembled forces to march on Kamakura, Yoshitoki countered by sending his own army under the leadership of his son Yasutoki. But he gave explicit orders that should the emperor himself be at the head of his army the shogunal troops must dismount and cut their bowstrings in sign of homage. Moreover, they were to accept unquestioningly whatever punishment the emperor saw fit to impose. Though apparently contradictory, Yoshitoki's attitude reflected a highly workable political ideology, on which the entire Japanese dual-power system is based. Yoshitoki knew that the inferior forces of the emperor were no match for his army. His intention was to put down Go-Toba once and for all and terminate imperial meddling in administrative matters. Still, he realized that insulting the authority of the emperor would upset the entire balance of the political system. As a matter of practical expediency, he simultaneously sent out an army to defeat Go-Toba and instructed his men to give way if the emperor himself rode in the van of his forces. After all, if his men did encounter Go-Toba and follow Yoshitoki's orders, the system would be served, and Yoshitoki would still have a chance another day to put the emperor back in his lofty, powerless place.

The story of Go-Toba and Yoshitoki reveals the basic Japanese belief that pragmatism and the preservation of harmonious human relations take pride of place over formal political codes of behavior. This belief springs from the religion Nihonism, which I shall discuss later. Here I would like to expand the idea of Japanese political pragmatism as illustrated in an interesting book called *Higurashi Suzuri* by Onda Moku (1711–62). Entrusted with the rehabilitation of the Yamashiro clan, whose lands were located in what is now Nagano Prefecture, Onda instituted a far-reaching system of reforms including installment-plan tax payments and public suggestion boxes in which the common people could deposit direct appeals to the clan lord.

During World War II, at the request of an American organization, I made a thorough study and translation of the book; and I consider it the best available text for an understanding of Japanese political thinking. It is short and concise; it is completely uninfluenced by European political philosophy; and since its author was not a man of letters but simply a skillful manager setting out to write a straightforward book, the text is direct and lacking in the complicated implications typical of much Japanese writing. Furthermore, since *Higurashi Suzuri* deals with the limited holdings of a small clan, the results of the policies adopted in it are as clear as if they had been produced in a laboratory test tube. Though Onda's methods and techniques are of a kind that no Jew or European would dream of employing, they are set forth with such clarity that anyone can readily understand them.

I have fond memories of this book, for I still own my old copy, one of a number that I bought and sent to the United States a few months before the opening of World War II. I intend to quote at length from the text of *Higurashi Suzuri,* but before I do, I must briefly sketch in the background of the situation with which it deals.

In 1756, floods and earthquakes so ravaged the lands of the Yamashiro clan that the inhabitants and the lord's family were in grave financial extremities. The vast sum they borrowed from the shogunate did not ease their situation. Ultimately all of the farmers in the area and, surprisingly, the foot soldiers as well, went on strike. (This may well be the first page in the history of strike movements in Japan.) At the time of Onda's story, the clan was headed by Sanada Yukitoyo, a bright young man who had become lord at the age of thirteen. To solve the serious difficulties that faced him in his sixteenth year, he singled out Onda, one of his humbler retainers, to straighten out the clan's financial affairs. Onda tried to decline the responsibility offered by Yukitoyo, but when he found that he would not be permitted to escape the task, he said that he would undertake it if the following conditions were met. First, he wanted a written clarification of his duties and rights. Second, no one was to be permitted to contradict him, and no one—neither the highest of the retainers nor any of the other clan officials—would be allowed to disobey his orders. In return for these conditions Onda set himself a five-year term of office and promised to face any punishment prescribed should he fail.

Upon returning home after his interview with the lord, Onda announced that henceforth he intended to take only light food and that he would order no new clothing. He further said that he would divorce his wife, disinherit his children, sever connections with his relatives, and let go all of the people he employed. When his surprised associates asked his reasons for these drastic measures, Onda said that he intended to speak only the truth in the future and that he could not afford to run the risk of being blamed for the chance slip or lie of a family member or employee. In short, he felt that he would be unable to carry out the needed reforms if so much as the shadow of a doubt about his veracity hung over him. But after having thought about what he said, all of his relatives and associates, vowing to limit their diets and to speak only the truth, pleaded with him to leave things as they were. On the basis of their promises, he relented. In taking this step, Onda obtained the confidence of his followers by assuring them that orders would not be arbitrarily altered and that things would always be done as promised.

Next Onda called all of the clan officials together and said that though payments of stipends had been in arrears or had sometimes failed entirely he intended to see that they were paid accurately in the future. In return he instituted a system of sure rewards and certain penalties. In other words, those who were careless in their public service would meet unfailing punishment. He then ordered village headmen, rich farmers, and police officials to gather and to bring with them people who could speak their minds well and clearly. On the appointed day, all of the officials, beginning with the chief retainers, assembled and sat in rows in the main hall. Onda Moku, after summoning certain representatives of the farmers, said as follows:

"I was called to Edo into the presence of our lord, with all of his relatives seated before him, and there I was ordered to assume the duties of financial controller of the lord's domain. Although I requested permission to decline, it was not granted, and I have therefore accepted the task. I do not, however, think that my strength alone is sufficient. For that reason I have called you together to discuss this matter. First I ask that you listen to what I have to say; then you may all say what you want.

"I realize that because of the lord's financial predicament many of you have been caused a great deal of trouble. It may well be that in the future, as I attempt to fulfill my role as financial controller, you will be caused still further trouble, and for that I am sorry. But first of all I promise to propose nothing that is impossible; once I have made a statement I will not alter it. I want you to understand this clearly. Further, unless you and I discuss all matters openly with each other, it will be impossible to put the clan's financial situation in order. Since I cannot succeed by myself, I ask that all of you talk everything over with me freely. This is my first request of you.

"Next, if you are not convinced that what I am doing is right, my work becomes impossible; and I will have no recourse but to commit suicide as custom demands. Whether I am able to do my work smoothly and successfully or whether I must kill myself as a result of failure depends on you. Please let me hear what your feelings are on this point. Of course, I realize that it may be difficult for you to answer now and in this place. Answer me after you have returned to your villages and have talked the matter over with the other farmers."

Then all of the farmers present said that, since in the past the falsehoods of officials and arbitrary alteration of instructions and information had caused them much distress, they were all extremely happy to hear Onda's proposed policy. Onda in turn replied that he was most satisfied that everyone was convinced. He then continued:

"Next, not only on auspicious occasions but also at all other times, I will allow no sending of gifts, no matter how inexpensive. I will not term such gifts bribes, since that would create difficulties for everyone."

On hearing this, all the farmers said that this was a greater blessing than they had expected. Onda went on to say the following:

"In the future I intend to hear everyone's requests and pleas; therefore, there is no need to send bribes to anyone. This goes for all officials as well as for the farmers.

"The next point concerns tax collection. In the past, one hundred from each one thousand available foot soldiers have been kept in the castle for various jobs. Each month the remaining nine hundred were sent to the villages to collect tribute rice. But from now on this practice will cease. Will this cause you distress?"

To this the farmers replied that nothing could make them happier than to be relieved of the burden of the foot-soldier tax collectors who had been in the habit of bringing trouble and violence to the villages during the five or seven days they spent as gatherers of tribute rice. On this point too everyone agreed and found satisfaction. Onda continued:

"Although it is difficult to predict the distant future, I intend to fill this office for five years. During that time, I will levy no demands on you for regional construction or for various duties in the castle. Will it distress you to be relieved of these duties?"

To this all those present answered that the relief from a variety of corvées only increased their happiness.

Onda then said that he wanted all present to remember carefully that they had agreed to and were satisfied with everything he had proposed up to this point. The next matter would require considerable discussion. Onda then said that he knew that among those present were some farmers who had paid advance tribute rice and in some cases even advances on the advances. He asked why they had done so, and the farmers replied that though it caused them hardship to meet these demands the officials had ordered it, and they, the farmers, merely did as they were commanded. They had no way out of the predicament. Onda, on the other hand, said that even in the face of the officials' orders the farmers would have been correct to refuse to pay anything but the tribute due for the current year.

"Taxes paid are over and done with, and certainly there

should be no need to pay in advance. You farmers were foolish to give in so readily, and the officials were cruel and even more foolish than you to rely on your easy compliance with their orders.

"This of course is only abstract theory. In fact, it was the poor financial condition of the clan that made it necessary for the officials to demand advances and advances on advances. Cruelty and avarice were not behind the orders. And you farmers, realizing that it was for the clan's sake and not for that of the officials, paid the taxes, though it distressed you to do so."

He praised all the farmers who had paid advances for being honest and straightforward in their devotion to the clan and said that the lord of such a clan of faithful followers was fortunate indeed.

He then called forth all those who had made loans to the clan and asked whether they had done it as the result of a desire to make profit by charging interest. These men, however, said that far from making interest on their loans, they had not succeeded in getting back their principal.

Onda said: "Is that the way it was? If you had said, however, that you did not have the money, even if the order to lend it had come from Edo itself, you could have gone to the city and refused to lend on the basis of your lack. The government would not have been within its rights to execute you for your refusal. The local officials, however, went beyond the bounds of morality to demand money of you because they knew you had it and would lend if demanded, even though they had no way to repay it.

"This, again, is only in theory. The facts of the matter are these: the clan is in such financial straits that it is impossible for us to fulfill our appointed duties in Edo.

Realizing this, though aware that you would not get the money back, you lent what you had. Thanks to you, we were able to do our duty in Edo. You did not lend because of the strict insistence of the collecting officials but because you knew it would make possible the successful completion of the necessary duties in Edo. You have not been repaid because the clan does not have the money. Our lord is grateful to you for having made his success possible, but in the future, no more loans will be required."

For this all the farmers expressed their thanks, and Onda said that he was pleased they were all in accord with him.

"Now there are some of you who have not paid your taxes for some time. Why? In general, farmers who sow seed and fertilize the land and perform all other agricultural duties at the proper time are able to lead good lives with their families and to pay their tribute rice as is expected of them. Is it that you who have not paid did not work enough to scrape together the required tribute? Are you so lazy as this, even when there are others who have paid their taxes two years in advance? People of such impudence are detestable to the extent that I could see them cut into small pieces and still not appease my anger at their behavior. And why did the officials allow these evaders to get away with their tricks? They should have wrenched the tribute from them by any means at hand."

Throughout this speech Onda's face flamed with such anger that all the people present bowed their heads.

"But this too is only in theory. For when it was known that the lord's finances were in bad condition and that there were those who had lent and others who had paid advances on their taxes, people who failed to pay what was expected of them were doubtless the victims of extreme poverty. I am certain that these people too wanted to pay their taxes quickly, but because of long sickness or misfortune they were unable to till the soil properly and therefore had no income. In addition, the officials, taking pity on these people, allowed them to fall into payment arrears without punishment. This is an instance of great sympathy on their part, for which we must be grateful. They realized that no amount of coercion could squeeze the tribute from people who did not have the funds with which to pay. The lack of payment must then become the clan's and the lord's loss and the gain of those who did not pay. Be informed, then, that all unpaid taxes to this point are forgiven. But anyone who fails to pay this year's tributes, though he be stark naked with poverty, will face a punishment worse than death."

All present expressed their understanding and agreement. Onda continued:

"Although we should like to return the advances and the advances on advances that some of you have paid, we lack the funds to do so. Furthermore, as you have heard, we intend to forgive all taxes in arrears to this point. Therefore, I request that all of you who have paid advances accept the loss."

All present anwered that they understood and that if, as Onda had promised, no advance payments were to be demanded in the future, they agreed to write off as loss all of the advances they had paid to that date.

"It makes me extremely happy that you see eye to eye with me. But I have one more request. As I said before, I do not want you to answer me now. Instead I want you to return to your villages and tell the other farmers what I have said. All of you must deliberate on the question together before returning an answer. If you fail to agree, I must commit suicide. Remember that the things I request are these: all advances paid to the present must be written off as losses in favor of the clan, and everyone must pay this year's tax rice without fail. There are some things to take into consideration, however, that make the picture brighter than you might think. I am sure that you have given the matter close calculation, and so have I. Do not forget that all bribes that were customarily paid in the past have been forbidden. This alone will save the villages about 100 *koku** of rice a year. In addition, the foot soldiers who formerly made monthly trips to collect taxes will no longer be lodged on you. This means great savings in the housing and food that you provided. Furthermore, you will no longer be forced to supply people and funds for duties and services to officials. All the savings the eliminations of these burdens bring to the farmers will amount to about seventy percent of this year's tax assessment. In addition, starting now I should like to put tribute taxes for the Yamashiro clan on a monthly installment basis.

"Whether my work leads to success or to my suicide depends on your willingness to accept my proposals. Please return to your villages and discuss the matter earnestly."

The farmers replied that they were ready to answer immediately but that in accordance with Onda's request they would return to their villages to explain this benevolent and superb plan to their fellow farmers. They felt certain that the plan would be happily received and that they would bring back a favorable answer.

"To those who lent money to the clan," Onda went on,

---

* A *koku* is about five bushels.

"we should like to return what we owe; but we do not have the funds at present. It may be that some of your children or grandchildren will find themselves in financial troubles or in hard times in the future. We should like to pay the money back to them when it becomes needed, but we will be unable to pay interest. All we can return is the principal. Probably none of you will fail without the return of the loans at the present. For this reason I ask you to lend it to the clan and to leave it with the clan until your children or grandchildren need it. This too is a request that I make of you all."

To this the farmers who had lent money said that since they had lent it with the intention of helping the clan they did not expect any of it back. But they said that they were very happy and grateful to accept this kind and generous offer on behalf of their children and grand-children. They said they would be indebted to the clan for this kindness, and some of them even wept as they expressed their gratitude.*

Once again Onda expressed his happiness that everyone agreed with him. He then said if any of them had been in-jured or harmed in any way during the past period of bad po-litical administration they might unhesitatingly write down their complaints, which they might present after sealing them well. The farmers, after stating that they understood, went happily on their way home. The officials, who had been seated in silent attention, blanched at the mention of permission to submit written complaints. There were even some present who thought it advisable to get rid of Onda.

* It is clearly wrong to regard the clan's attitude as cavalier and the farmers as gullible: after all no such rapport existed between the French aristocrats and peasants at the time of the Revolution.

Then the farmers who had returned to the villages called together their fellows and explained Onda's proposal point by point. The farmers were delighted. They said that the relief they would have from the irksome tax-collecting forages of the foot soldiers was so great a blessing that, in combination with the savings resulting from the removal of duties in connection with the officials and the castle, it would enable them to pay with ease far more taxes than were demanded. Then they insisted that they deliver an answer of agreement as quickly as possible because they wanted to put both Onda's and the lord's mind at rest.

Then the village headmen and the work foremen, in their greetings to the groups, said: "We must hurry to the public office and make known everyone's agreement to Onda's proposal. It will look better for us if we go quickly." Everyone was overjoyed at this, and they then decided to compose the complaints about former abuses that Onda had instructed them to write. Everyone was in the best of moods, for the time had come for them to make clear all the things they had suffered and hated in the past. It was as if a bright moon had suddenly appeared to illuminate the darkest night. There was happiness in each man's heart, for he felt that in the future everything would certainly go well.

After the complaints had been written and the farmers had discussed things among themselves, the village head-men and the leaders of the farmers departed for the public office, where they made the following report:

"When we told the farmers of the proposals, they were overjoyed and grateful. We have resolved to offer to pay two years' advance taxes and to lend other money whenever you may order it as a result of your needs. Please understand our willingness to do these things."

But Onda replied: "Thanks to you, the farmers have agreed. This means that I will be able to fulfill my task without committing suicide. It is thanks to all the farmers. Moreover, when the lord hears that you have willingly offered to pay two years' tribute rice in advance, it will certainly bring him great satisfaction. But it will be sufficient for you to pay only this year's taxes. Your feelings are too profound. I shall tell our lord that you will pay this year's taxes, but there is no need to make an advance.

"On the other hand, you must all work as hard as you can. I am sure that I need not say this, but to do less than your best at your farming tasks is a sin against heaven. Work with diligence at your farming, and do what you like with the time that is left over. In your leisure, indulge in ballad singing, playing the samisen, or gambling; but remember that gambling for money is illegal and that anyone caught at it is liable to the death penalty. As long as no money transactions are involved, it is all right to gamble. In general, unless people have some suitable recreation for their leisure hours their work will be less effective than it ought to be. For that reason I order you to enjoy yourselves but to work with all your might, too.

"Finally, remember that people who do not believe in the Buddhas and the gods are bound to suffer great hardships. Therefore it is good to believe and to pray for both this world and the world to come.

"Now, did you bring the complaints I told you to write?" asked Onda; and the farmers' representatives replied that they had. Onda then said that they were not for his eyes and that he would present them to the lord. With this he told the farmers to return to their homes and to work with all their might.

He then hastened to the lord, to whom he said: "Please rejoice, for the financial situation is certain to improve. The farmers have agreed to cancel our debts to them. This means that we owe nothing. And starting this month they will pay a full ten thousand koku in rice as taxes. Because they have agreed to pay everything to the very last grain, our financial recovery is certain. No one holds anything against the clan. On the contrary, they are so happy that they volunteered to pay two years' taxes instead of one. I am convinced that it is because of your great kindness and moral virtues that the farmers have consented to go along with my policies and to pay their taxes promptly and accurately."

The lord answered: "No, it is because of your efforts. You have been a faithful retainer worthy of the highest reward." After thanking the lord for his praises, Onda said: "It is now time to examine the petitions containing the farmers' complaints. Please examine them for yourself." And with this he handed them over to the lord.

Later, the lord summoned Onda and said to him: "Look at the complaints that the farmers living in my domain have written. This is what they wrote." And Onda replied after examining the materials: "I knew that this was the kind of thing they would say." The lord then asked what he should do, and Onda answered: "There is no cause for worry. The farmers will adhere to one side or to the other. It depends on the way they are used. They will be good if a good person uses them, but they will be bad if a bad person uses them. Since you are a man of the highest morality and kindness, we have nothing to worry about. It is true that the officials against whom the farmers have complained deserve death for their wickedness, but since they are men of talent who are needful to us now, I suggest you call them before you and with a kind aspect instruct them in this way: tell them that though you have entrusted the financial recovery of the clan to me it is impossible for me to attend to all details. Therefore, they must help me in my tasks. Tell them too that they must follow my instructions and, doing their work in agreement with my wishes, discuss all things with me."

The lord then asked if such a step would not interfere with the successful accomplishment of Onda's own work. Onda denied that it would hinder him in any way. After saying that he would do as Onda wished, the lord called in his officials and with a mild face instructed them as Onda had said. To these instructions they all agreed gratefully and readily, according to the *Higurashi Suzuri*.

Having been requested to do a translation of this book because of my skill in Japanese, I resolved to give the committee who would review my work a thoroughly annotated text. After I had submitted my manuscript, I met with the committee for a question-and-answer period. I shall never forget the surprise and shock the contents of the Onda Moku text brought to the faces of the people assembled. Clearly they were all wondering how to begin the questioning because from their standpoint Onda's actions were theoretically illogical and unfair. For instance, in some cases he condoned advance land-tax payments and even advances on advances, whereas in others he asked for nothing at all. Moreover, people who accepted bribes profited by doing so, since no penalties were prescribed. The committee members could not understand that such an administration could be taken as an example of "benevolent rule."

The one Jewish member of the panel asked a question—one I would have expected of him—that showed me the way to deal with the objections being raised. He asked: "In effecting his reforms, on what law did Onda Moku base his actions and how did he interpret that law?" This seemed typical of Jewish thinking, which works from the abstract rule to the particular instance. Jews believe that justice and fairness must spring from principles more reliable and trustworthy than fallible human judgment. In the history of the Jewish people, all political actions were—or more accurately ought to have been—founded on the Law of God. Obviously backsliding was not uncommon, but the thundering utterances of the great prophets of the Old Testament bear witness to the ever-present conviction that things went wrong if they were contrary to God's Law.

The complaints from the other committee members, though inspired by different traditions, were also related to the question of abstract principle. The others felt that it was wrong for inequality to be condoned. They could not understand why advance land taxes should be taken from some people while no payments were required of others. The American mind reasons that if unfair tax practices result from faults in the tax laws, those laws need revision. If tax evasion exists—as it did in the Onda Moku story—the evaders must be forced to pay. Finally, the idea of allowing those who accepted bribes to escape without questioning, even in the face of proof of their guilt, runs counter to all American concepts of reason and morality.

What all of these objectors overlooked was the simple fact

that they were thinking in terms of abstract theory, whereas Onda specifically renounced theory as inapplicable to the practical exigencies of the case he had to deal with. The only laws he had to base his actions on were those of pragmatism and the preservation of harmonious human relations. Although he realized that everyone ought to pay his taxes, some of the clansmen simply could not pay. From those who had money he demanded more because this was the way to acquire the requisite funds. Although to Western minds his actions seem inconsistent in the extreme, they are based on a logic beyond ordinary logic, which every Japanese understands and employs in almost all decisions.

The Jewish member argued that Onda's actions ought to be based on law; the non-Jewish members stood up for logic and fairness. But Onda himself abandoned abstract law and formal logic for a flexibility that enabled him to solve, smoothly and pacifically, complicated difficulties that the application of ordinary laws and reason would only aggravate. His efforts succeeded because the people he controlled took this approach for granted. Onda nonetheless clarified his position before both his lord and his subordinates. (The late Prime Minister Ikeda had to do likewise after the finalization of the Security Treaty between Japan and the United States in 1960.) Onda then gained the trust of his people by demonstrating his trust in them. Indeed he went so far as to say that without their cooperation he would fail and that failure would necessitate his suicide. In short, Onda appealed to their humanity, the foundation of Nihonism.

The entire Japanese nation is a body of faithful followers of Nihonism, which is based on human experience instead of on a covenant or body of dogma. Hojo Yoshitoki intuitively felt, if he did not rationally recognize, this religious faith as the foundation of the dual-power system. The Jews, the Crusaders, the Company of the Saints, the Americans, the Soviet Russians, and Milovan Djilas consider the goal of politics to be the realization of an absolute or divine justice. But the Japanese concern themselves entirely with concrete goals. In the case of Onda Moku, the goal was the financial rehabilitation of the clan. He would stretch any ruling to the breaking point in order to attain his end. Today any Japanese politician who fails to understand and apply this pragmatic approach is doomed to failure at home no matter how highly he may be regarded abroad. It is because most Japanese politicians have always grasped the meaning of the logic beyond logic and the importance of pragmatic action that the nation has been able to effect surprising reforms while preserving political stability.

It is rarely advisable to follow the advice of geniuses, who always underrate their own abilities and think that others ought to succeed wherever they themselves can. When I was a boy living in Kobe one of my schoolmates was a mathematical genius. In the hopes of improving my own poor grades in this subject, I solicited my friend's advice. He assured me that all I needed to do was to stop preparing my lessons and simply come to class. If I did this, he claimed, correct answers to all problems would pop into my head of their own accord. Needless to say, the answers did nothing of the kind, and my mathematics grades took a startling plunge. Sometimes in moments of reverie I think how much more quickly the Jews would have regained their ancient homeland if they had had the political pragmatism to play all sides off against one another as the Japanese have done in bringing about the reversion of Okinawa. But, unfortunately, genius in pragmatic politics is peculiar to the Japanese, and other people attempting to copy their methods will fare no better than I did in following the advice of my schoolmate.

6. *Divine Law, Human Law*

It can be argued that the Cruci-
fixion was illegal, since the Sanhedrin, the supreme judicial
and legislative body of the Jews, in unanimously condemn-
ing Christ to death, ignored its own rule that unanimous
trial verdicts were invalid. The breaking of this rule was
more than a flaw in legal procedures, however: it amounted
to a violation of the relationship between man and God
that lay at the heart of Jewish society. Man is finite, God
infinite, and from these antithetical conditions is generated
a synthesis that takes the form of absolute obedience to
God's will. Included in this synthesis is a recognition
that the kind of perfection implied by unanimous verdicts
is a divine attribute; thus the Sanhedrin erred grievously
in the manner in which it handled the condemnation of
Christ.

I do not believe that most Jews are conscious of how obedience to the law is an outcome of those forces which shaped the synthesis, but an awareness was indirectly expressed by the Minor Prophet Micah, who lived in the eighth century B.C. An independent farmer residing in Morasheth, a village about twenty miles southwest of Jerusalem, where the land was rich and suited to the raising of wheat, Micah one day heard the call of God and became a prophet. If the words attributed to him in the Bible are correct, he advocated a number of ideas that were later incorporated into Jewish life.

For example, Micah asserted that the Temple was built by the blood of the poor, whom the powerful had ruthlessly exploited to obtain money for its glorification. As I have noted, obedience to God's law is the inevitable result of the fundamental relationship between God and man. By committing wicked acts, even if ostensibly for the sake of God's glorification, those who robbed the poor to build the Temple broke the law and were subject to divine punishment.

Micah says: "Woe to those who devise wickedness and work evil upon their beds! When morning dawns, they perform it, because it is in the power of their hand. They covet fields, and seize them; and houses, and take them away; they oppress a man and his house, a man and his inheritance." (Mic. 2: 1–2)

And: "Hear this, you heads of the house of Jacob and rulers of the house of Israel, who abhor justice and pervert all equity, who build Zion with blood and Jerusalem with wrong. . . . Therefore because of you Zion shall be plowed as a field; Jerusalem shall become a heap of ruins, and the mountain of the house a wooded height." (Mic. 3: 9–10, 12)

And later: "And in that day, says the Lord, I will cut off your horses from among you and will destroy your chariots; and I will cut off the cities of your land and throw down all of your strongholds. . . ." (Mic. 5: 10–11)

The doctrine that man's acts must be referred to divine law permeates the writings of Jewish thinkers and has become an integral part of the substance of the Jewish people. The Apostle Paul illustrates the operation of this belief with an interesting variation. As Saul, the ardent Pharisee student of Gamaliel, he saw man's duty as obedience to the Laws of Moses. After being blinded on the road to Damascus and hearing the voice of Jesus of Nazareth, Saul's meeting in Damascus with Ananias, who restored his sight, led him to conversion and baptism. He then recognized the teachings of Christ as the new rule by which human actions must be regulated. He did not abandon the idea of a synthesis born of the relation between man and God, but he did reinterpret the nature of that synthesis. He felt that Christ had freed humanity from the old law but had provided a different though no less binding set of controls. This approach could not be condoned by orthodox Jews, however, for from their standpoint it is man's place to abide by and not willfully to alter God's law.

To return to the Sanhedrin for a moment, its procedures reflected a belief that unanimity of human judgment suggests absolute rightness and, in a sense, amounts to the usurpation of a divine attribute. The Sanhedrin was arguing, then, that its seventy members could not agree with each other unless induced to do so by outside pressures, bribery, or exceptional emotional circumstances. When a unanimous decision occurred in cases of capital punishment, it was customary to postpone proceedings for further deliberation or to hold a retrial. As the Sanhedrin did not do either of these things in the case of Christ, but sentenced him at once and unanimously to death, they made a serious mistake by their own standards.

In contrast to the Jewish distrust of unanimous verdicts and decisions, the Japanese are highly in favor of them. Still, when they evaluate what happened at Christ's trial, the Sanhedrin's disbelief in unanimous decisions isn't what intrigues them. Rather, they tend to conclude that the decision itself reveals how corrupt humanity can be, since Christ was clearly an innocent victim of circumstances. Generally, however, the Japanese believe that unanimity signifies harmonious relations among all parties. It is therefore greatly to be desired. Indeed, the appearance of unanimity is often created by the Japanese when in fact there may be serious discord among the involved parties. In a business firm, for example, a written proposal may be circulated for review and comment to everyone connected with its implementation. Generally, each man involved will read it and affix his signature seal to the paper to indicate approval. When the document leaves the desk of the senior manager, it apparently has the stamp of agreement of everyone concerned, even though one or more persons may have in fact been against it. Nevertheless, the appearance of concord has been achieved, and this is considered to be good because it results in collective responsibility for the success or failure of the measures described in the proposal. Subsequent developments may well show that the proposal was impractical, that many who ostensibly went

along with it really didn't approve, and that major altera-
tions were essential. Why, then, do the Japanese favor
unanimous decisions in form although well aware that some
individuals may be secret dissenters?

The answer is that to their way of thinking a unanimous
decision is as good as any in theory because no rule is valid
unless it conforms to a synthesis they have evolved from the
relationship between man and the exigencies of existence.
The Jews, as I have noted, regard obedience to divine law
as the inevitable outcome of the God-man relation; the
Japanese, on the other hand, believe in a law that transcends all codified law, and one that demands flexibility of
attitude and adaptability to the human circumstances of
the moment rather than unquestioning obedience to some
abstract principle.

Though the Japanese argue that majority decisions are
what make their nation run, they treat the laws and regulations resulting from such decisions in a revealing way.
The rule of thumb seems to be that a man chooses to obey
or disobey a law on the basis of the extent to which it ac-
cords with the facts of human existence. A much publicized
event illustrating this attitude occurred during the year
after World War II, when a prohibited black market in rice
flourished. Food was so scarce that few Japanese—neither
the Diet members who passed the legislation outlawing the
black market nor the judges responsible for sentencing
violators of the law—hesitated to purchase illegal rice. One
judge, however, was reported in the popular press to have
literally starved to death because he refused to break the
law. Public reactions to his adamant stand were instruc-
tive: some people praised the judge for his principles; others
criticized him for impracticality. After all, a man must eat,

and rules are made to be broken if they run counter to human needs.

To Jews, the Japanese willingness to obey or disobey laws as circumstances and convenience dictate is basically unintelligible. On the other hand, the Japanese regard the complicated regulations governing the lives of orthodox Jews as excessively strict and almost ludicrous in their irrelevance to what the Japanese consider the basic human experience. Similarly, the impersonal nature of certain court proceedings in the United States strikes the Japanese as silly. A person tried and convicted on several counts may be given a string of sentences amounting to ninety-nine or more years. According to the law, each crime carries a certain punishment and the law must be applied as written. From the Japanese standpoint this is meaningless, since people simply do not live long enough to serve, say, a century in jail.

Quite obviously, if everyone in a society is free to interpret the law as he sees fit, chaos results. But Japanese society works efficiently because everyone in the nation understands the pragmatic principles that give final strength and shape to law. These principles derive from what might best be expressed as "human experience." The Japanese word *ningen,* or humanity, is widely used and is apt to turn up anywhere, like the joker in a deck of playing cards. A judge's verdict may be described as "full of humanity," or a good person may be "richly human," of "mature humanity," and "truly human." A bad person is "inhuman," or "does not seem human at all." Examples of this usage are unlimited because all laws in Japan are evaluated on the basis of how well they fit or do not fit the facts of men's lives. Not abstract or theoretical law, but only that which appears proper in the light of human experience, is considered legal and binding on all.

This unwritten law of humanity extends to every phase of Japanese life. When making judgments, courts must turn their attention to such questions as: Was the accused under unusual stress at the time of the crime? Had he suffered an especially embittering childhood? Is he now repentant and willing to lead a good life hereafter? If a court evaluates such factors, it is thought to have acted wisely, or humanely. If it does not, no matter that its verdict follows the written law to the last letter, the Japanese consider it unfair.

The decisions and acts of lawmaking bodies too are weighed according to similar criteria. The decree forbidding the purchase of black-market rice prevented people from obtaining the most important staple food for their families. Consequently, the ruling could be broken. This permissive attitude did not extend to the operators of the black market, however, because they were making private profit out of human misery and therefore deserved punishment.

Today the unwritten law operates in the complicated and never-ending struggle between the tax authorities and the taxpayers. As was noted in the first chapter of this book, the Japanese find the government's need of money to provide national defense and to maintain essential services unpalatable. They feel as if they were being robbed of something rightly their own, or, put in another way, as if they were being treated in an inhuman manner. For this reason, they not only resent but also evade taxes, justifying themselves by the dictates of the unwritten law that what interferes with human needs is violable. Tax officials are human too and, instead of applying sanctions severely, generally reach some kind of accommodation with transgressors. As a matter of fact, if they did otherwise, most Japanese would be before the courts for tax evasion.

By way of recapitulation, I will summarize what has been said to this point. Jews think in terms of an antithetical relation between fallible humanity and infallible God. The synthesis generated from these opposites is a divinely ordained, infallible, therefore immutable law, which man must obey without question. In their view of the world, the Japanese too recognize a thesis—man—and an antithesis. But the latter is not a divine god but the facts, the exigencies of human experience and life. These two generate a synthesis in the form of what is really a law beyond the law. It is not divine; therefore, it makes no claims to infallibility or immutability. On the contrary, its chief characteristic is its flexibility and conformability to prevailing circumstances. I think I have illustrated how this doctrine works in the preceding chapter on the Japanese pragmatic view of political activities. But this law beyond the law permeates all Japanese life to assume the status of a faith that is, in my estimation, as much a religion as Judaism, Christianity, or Islam.

Many foreigners think that the Japanese are irreligious, for the practice of religion is taken lightly in Japan. But the true national religion, the one that governs everything the Japanese do or think, is in fact extremely demanding. I have already mentioned this religion, which I call Nihonism, in connection with the reforms of Onda Moku, but there is no aspect of life in Japan that it does not affect or control. Everything the Japanese do must be judged by its precepts, which are ultimately sanctioned by the unwritten law that transcends all legal codes. As I have said, however, this unwritten law itself must conform to prevailing human circumstances. In spite of the Japanese fondness for reassuring unanimous agreements—or at least the appearance of such—decisions in which everyone concurs must be altered if they fall short of the requirements of Nihonism. It follows, then, that since nothing can be absolutely certain because the human condition is constantly changing, the Japanese avoid taking fixed stands on issues. It is true that desperate fanatics and radical student activists are tolerated; they too are part of the human drama. By believing that what is true today may be false tomorrow, the Japanese adopt an apparent impartiality and refuse to reach definite conclusions. This attitude makes Westerners feel most insecure.

The lack of fixed stands on issues is clearly reflected in the Japanese national press. In most countries, newspapers and magazines have definite editorial stances that permit readers to orient themselves and to have adequate means by which to judge the opinions of a writer. In Japan, this is rare, although a few newspapers, such as the conservative *Nihon Keizai Shimbun* (Japan Economic Journal) or the Communist *Akahata* (Red Banner) do advocate readily identifiable points of view. But most of the vernacular press is, in this respect, an almost impenetrable riddle to a non-Japanese, because the usual writer merely reports on vital issues without comment. His newspaper does not ask him for an evaluation; he himself does not feel the need to provide one. As a good Nihonist, he does not want to be branded a heretic.

In the West, impartiality is often thought of as a divine attribute. Because of their fallibility, men must make judgments, and societies require established codes of ethics. By this reckoning, the typical Japanese newspaper is shirking its duties. The Japanese, on the other hand, feel that humanity is well served by avoiding judgments. In this they are faithful adherents of Nihonism and true exponents of a set of beliefs that bases all law and conduct of men's affairs upon the mutability of the human condition. Human law takes precedence over divine law.

7. *Unique and Exclusive*

A PERSON IS JAPANESE OR JEWISH BY birth, and in the strictest sense no one can "become" one or the other. My own case is an illustration of my meaning. I am a Jew by birth; I would have been a Jew no matter where I was born. As it turned out I was born in Kobe, Japan, but this event did not make me Japanese either in the eyes of the people of Japan or in the legal sense. Had I been born a Jew in the United States, no matter what the national background of my family, I would have been an American citizen. Such is not the case in Japan, but this has little bearing on the true nature of Japaneseness, since even citizenship is unimportant in determining who is truly Japanese.

I once had a Japanese friend who was a talented painter. Before World War II he married a Frenchwoman, who subsequently was granted Japanese citizenship. One day

I mentioned to another friend that the painter's wife had been French but was now Japanese. This friend immediately jumped to the conclusion that the painter had divorced his French wife to marry a Japanese. To his way of thinking, becoming Japanese was an impossibility no matter what citizenship a person possessed. His reaction was not exceptional. During the war, military police called on the painter to investigate his alien wife. They were startled to learn that—legally at any rate—she was Japanese. What they saw was an outsider *(gaijin)*, who, like myself, could never be made into an insider. This Japanese attitude goes so far that the descendants of Korean craftsmen brought to Japan 300 years ago by Shimazu Yoshihiro of Kagoshima are still aliens. Like the Jews, the Japanese believe in their uniqueness. But the Japanese have an interesting blind spot about the uniqueness of the Jews. For example, during the Six-Day War a Japanese journalist writing for a progressive magazine postulated that no such thing as a Jew exists: all people calling themselves Jews are in fact French, German, English, and so on, depending upon the country in which they live. (His argument gave me a start, for the writer was denying the very existence of Jews; earlier the Nazis did all they could to wipe the Jews out of existence.) Although the writer would have considered a Jew born in France a Frenchman, I doubt that he would have allowed me the honor of being Japanese, in spite of my having been born in Kobe.

More than anything else, the Diaspora forced the Jews into an intensified sense of identity and, perhaps, excessive consciousness of being part of a particular religious faith. Scattered over many parts of the globe, yet united by the idea of the synagogue and by rabbinical tradition, Jews could not avoid comparing themselves with the peoples among whom they lived. In doing so, they discovered their own traits, from which evolved an awareness of a unique thing called Jewishness. The Japanese, never having undergone such dispersal, are less aware of the forces that unite them, especially of that great binding faith which I have called Nihonism. It has so permeated the minds of its followers that it is taken for granted, a remarkable fact when one considers that it is as valid a religion as Judaism, Christianity, or Islam.

Like other religions, Nihonism may be divided into certain branches or factions. At present it seems to me that the following exist: Christian, Soka Gakkai (Nichiren Buddhist), Marxist, and Humanist Capitalist (represented by a "Peace and Happiness through Prosperity" movement). These large groupings can be subdivided into smaller factions, some of which are extremist and radical in nature. Luckily most people pay little attention to issues that incense extremists. Instead they try to live their lives within the boundaries of traditional, often religious, beliefs. In Japan these beliefs are those of Nihonism, which extends to all phases of human activity.

Surely it is futile to attempt to transform a faith as deeply rooted as Nihonism into another religion, yet Christian missionaries have long pursued this tragicomic course. Their major mistake is one that is hard to credit in light of the means by which Christianity has triumphed in other parts of the world. Generally speaking, the great leaders of the early Christian Church recognized and made effective use of aspects of other faiths that they overcame. The selection of the date of a pagan Roman festival as the time of the Christmas celebration is only one of the many illustrations of this process. In Japan, on the other hand, the missionaries have compeletely overlooked a wealth of religiously founded custom and belief that they might have turned to good use. They have erred on this point probably because they, like many others including some of the Japanese themselves, have swallowed the fallacy that the Japanese are basically an irreligious people. But no purely irreligious human exists. Most men hold to some faith, even if it does not take the form of organized religion. And the Japanese, as I have argued, are devoted—if often unaware—followers of Nihonism.

To missionaries setting out to convert the Japanese I often say that they ought first to familiarize themselves with the works of literature that in Nihonism correspond to the Gospel of John, the Book of Genesis, Isaiah, and the Epistle to the Romans. When the would-be proselytizers recover from the unsettling discovery that works of this kind exist, I tell them that for a deeper knowledge of the people they intend to convert they ought to study the lives of the martyrs of Nihonism. At this the missionaries usually look incredulous. But what religion does not have its martyrs? Alarm does not abate when I name Saigo Takamori as one of these martyrs. (I shall discuss this samurai and leader in the next chapter, but suffice it to say here that he is an outstanding example of martyrdom to Nihonism.) I then try to console the missionaries: "Don't worry. Go ahead with your preaching for a few decades, and when you are older, Japanese are likely to say something like this about you: 'That man is a missionary, but he doesn't seem like one at all. He is a fine person with a rich sense of humanity.'" The word "humanity" is the key, for the missionary is being treated as a member of the Christian branch of Nihonism, the central element of which is humanity, not a god. Though unknowingly, the missionary has in effect become part of another religion; the Japanese remain unconverted.

Since humanity, not a deity, sits at the center of Nihonism, its Book of Genesis might read something like this: "Neither the spirit nor God created the world of man. Rather it was made by the neighbors on both sides and the people living in the three houses on the other side of the street. [This is the Japanese way of describing a neighborhood.] The world of man may be hard to live in, but there is no other land to flee to. And even if such a land did exist, it would be inhuman, therefore more difficult to live in than the world of man. If this inescapable world of man becomes difficult, make the best of it. Live out the brief span of life as comfortably as possible. To help us all do this we have the heaven-appointed poets and artists, whose duty is to make the world of man tranquil and to enrich the human heart."

The celebrated twentieth-century novelist and great intellectual Soseki Natsume, who was well versed in the classics of the West, Japan, China, and Buddhism, believed that man made man's world. His works reflect this conviction in that they explain everything in terms of humanity. One of his earliest and best known books, *I Am a Cat* (Wagahai wa Neko De-aru), satirizes people and society by revealing them as seen through the eyes of a cat protagonist. The cat becomes a kind of ruling spirit; there are no gods in the book at all. In the Old Testament, God is the ruling spirit; and there are no cats. It is possible for Natsume to envisage a godless world overseen by an omniscient cat, whereas in the world of the Old Testament, the Divinity knows everything, though cats are notably lacking. These then are two completely contrasting interpretations of the world—one completely human and one governed by a godhead—and only a madman would attempt to live in both simultaneously.

If *I Am a Cat* is related to Nihonism's Genesis, another of Natsume's works, a great short story called *Kusamakura* (Grass Pillow), deserves attention as resembling Isaiah in its condemnation of the world and prophecy of grave troubles. The philosophy on which the story is based, however, centers entirely on mankind. Natsume writes: "The world is pesky, poisonous, fidgety, and nervy into the bargain. It is packed full of rotten people. Some guys don't even know why they have pushed their mugs into this world. All they do know is that they want those mugs to be well known; a big name is all they are interested in. They think it's really the life to spend five or ten years chasing round other people's rear ends counting farts. Then they come right out in front of others with the unwanted information that 'You farted this many times or that many times.' Now if they told you to your face, it might serve some purpose, but they go around behind your back telling just how many farts you let. If you tell them they're noisy, they talk more. If you tell them to stop, they go on. And if you tell them you've got their message, they still tell how many times you farted. Then they claim that this is their way of getting on in the world. Of course, everyone has the right to get ahead as best he can, but it's better to do so without talking about other people's farts. It's only civil to make one's own way without causing trouble. If someone tells me that he cannot get along in this world without bothering others, then I'll have to use my own farts as a way of making my own way. When the situation comes to this, Japan is completely out of luck."

An imaginary Genesis and a Nihonistic view of the world lead me to the nature of communications within Nihonism. Before offering a possible recasting of the opening of the Gospel according to John, which deals with the nature of the word, let me first record a story that indicates much about the way the Japanese use words.

Many years ago a missionary came to Japan. One day he happened to see an old man standing reverently with hands clasped in prayer in front of a bronze statue of the Buddha. The missionary said to him: "God does not reside in things made of gold or bronze." Opening his eyes wide in surprise, the old man said: "Of course." It was then the missionary's turn to be surprised; he asked: "If you know that, why are you praying in front of this bronze statue?" The old man answered: "First one sweeps away the dust, then one looks at the Buddha. What is your answer?" The missionary stood silent, as the old man, after saying softly, "The Buddha is also dust," went away. Even if the missionary had tried to interpret the old man's question in the light of Christian teachings, I doubt if he would have found an answer. Both the partners in this chance encounter spoke in mutually unintelligible ways. The Japanese way was well expressed by the late novelist Yasunari Kawabata, who said, in an address delivered at the University of Hawaii, that the Japanese communicate by means of a quiet understanding, a kind of telepathy, since for them truth lies in the implied rather than the stated.

Kawabata's words lead one to an important point about Nihonism, one that can be elucidated by rewording the opening of the Gospel of John to read: "In the beginning was the implication (words beyond words), and the implication was with the word, and the word became the implication." Failure to grasp the importance of implications has caused many foreigners to complain that the Japanese never state their thoughts and conclusions clearly. I am afraid that this only reflects an inability to understand communications in the Japanese style. The world of the Japanese may be compared to non-Euclidean geometry. To attempt to apply Euclidean rules to it is to invite ridicule. Similarly, if one were to apply so-called common-sense logic to an exegesis of the Natsume passage about counting farts, a Japanese would listen politely and then, in his own way, create an exegesis of the exegesis.

The famous logic-wrenching word problems *(koan)* of Zen Buddhism involve extensive treatment and understanding of implication. Their subject matter is virtually unlimited; they may deal with Buddhist classics, bronze statues, a cat's neck, a sardine head, or even the Bible. In fact, members of the Christian branch of Nihonism are extremely skillful in applying words from the Scriptures to Zen-style koan. As translated into Japanese, the Bible is Zen-like, but the readings and interpretations of it are even more so. For example, a certain Japanese Christian minister considers Christ's encounter with Pilate in the Gospel of John to be a superb example of a koan. When Christ is before Pilate he says that he has come into the world to bear witness to the truth. Pilate asks: "What is truth?" and goes out. Although the minister's idea is original, it is also surprising. I am certain I find it so because I do not understand Nihonism well enough. A full understanding demands a complete command of the Japanese language, including a mastery of not only words but also implications. This is beyond my capabilities, and I cannot, therefore, condemn as wrong the Japanese teaching that the truth of the Bible is to be found between the lines and not in the text itself. Japanese accept only the implications of the Bible; but the implications are not the Bible.

One of the most difficult aspects of the entire situation is the fact that the concept of humanity lying at the heart of Nihonism cannot be expressed in words; it too relies upon implication for definition. Since a mastery of implications is impossible for foreigners, only Japanese can become Nihonists. When Rome destroyed Jerusalem, imperial soldiers broke into the Holy of Holies, but nothing, not even a nuclear bomb, can break into the inner sanctum of Nihonism. No foreigner can so much as approach it; all he can hope to do is to apprehend the world of words surrounding and protecting it. Something of its shape and texture can be grasped by looking closely at the Japanese, who are one people and one nation bound together by a single religion; by studying the lives and actions of historical figures who embody the meaning and practice of Nihonism; and by discerning the characteristic ways in which the followers of Nihonism interpret other religions. The rest of this chapter will be given over to further comments on the Japanese people as a whole, and in subsequent chapters I will deal with a singular case of a follower of Nihonism, and with Japanese ideas on other religions.

Though it sounds strange to Western ears, it is not at

all unusual in Japan to hear young engaged couples discussing whether their wedding ceremony will be Shinto,
Buddhist, or Christian. The nature of the rite makes no
difference, since those concerned are members of the Japan
faith I call Nihonism. In Israel, where there are followers
of Judaism, Islam, and Christianity, as well as some Druses,
the situation is quite different. Each religious group has
its own authorities who handle marriages, divorces,
adoptions, inheritances, and other domestic matters. In
some cases, there are first and second religious courts, and
a person dissatisfied with settlements handed down in
them may file an ordinary legal suit. In many ways, the
religious courts resemble Japanese domestic ones. In fact,
in order to prevent Japanese from interpreting the religious
court as something resembling an Inquisition tribunal, I
often cite the domestic court as its closest counterpart.
A single unified system of courts in Israel is out of the
question, given the separate religious codes—Rabbinical,
Christian, Drusian, and Islamic—found there. Though it
is natural that the regulations governing the lives of believers differ from religion to religion and must coexist
in countries like Israel and America, Japan is almost
unique in that its people, sharing a faith that transcends
all other religions, have no need of special bodies to pass
on matters relating specifically to Shinto, Buddhism, or
Christianity. A Japanese woman, a Christian and a graduate
of a mission school, may very well be married according
to Shinto rites, and her funeral service may be Buddhist.
This does not seem odd to the Japanese, nor does it indicate any lack of religious fastidiousness. Their apparently
eclectic approach to religious ceremony shows an indifference arising from the fact that at heart the only religion

they truly believe in is Nihonism. "Say what you like, when all is said and done, we are all Japanese," is a common remark. For "Japanese" in this statement, I would not hesitate to substitute "Nihonist."

The laws of most nations are based upon religious customs. If people abide by their own religious customs, there is rarely need to resort to troublesome litigation. Laws and religious codes, however, differ in at least one very important respect. Whereas the former may be repealed, altered, or amended to suit the needs of the times, the latter are generally regarded as sacrosanct and untouchable. Strangely enough, the history of national constitutions in Japan offers an interesting exception to how laws are usually treated.

Many Japanese today are vociferously outspoken against any revision of the nation's constitution, but their protests are scarcely warranted, since never in Japan's history has a constitution been revised. For example, when it was found by later authorities that the Taiho Code, first promulgated in 702, no longer met altered conditions, it was not revised. Instead the authorities simply established extra-legal governmental organs to handle situations beyond its range. A famous, and infamous, Police Commission (Kebiishicho) was one such organ. Interestingly enough, the modern Self-Defense Forces are an instance of the same kind of thing. One may search as diligently as possible without finding a single article in the present constitution authorizing the formation of a self-defense force. Ordinarily, when a people discover in their midst the existence of a non-constitutional armed body, they demand that the government immediately revise the constitution to bring this body under clear legal control.

I once suggested to a Japanese friend that it would be good to supplement the present constitution with an article stating the following: "The Self-Defense Forces shall be a provisional organization for the sake of defending the country. The limits of their actions shall be as follows. The Ground Self-Defense Forces shall be limited to the territory of the Japanese nation. The Maritime Self-Defense Forces shall be limited to the territorial waters of Japan and to specially designated international waters. The Air Self-Defense Forces shall be limited to the air spaces above the specified zones of activity of the Ground and Maritime Self-Defense Forces." I told my friend that to alter the constitution in this way would inspire a sense of security both in Japan and in neighboring countries and would thus help to lessen the danger of international misunderstanding. His answer was most illuminating: "Yes, you may be right; but in modern Japan one cannot lay hands on the constitution." What he was saying was not theory; it was fact. The Japanese never touch their constitutions. The Meiji Constitution, drawn up in the second half of the nineteenth century, was a code of laws designed to be valid for all times. The present constitution is the great document of peace. Both contain clauses dealing with revisions, but the provisions themselves are empty words dealing with a most unlikely contingency, because the constitutions of Japan are not legal codes but religious classics of Nihonism.

Even sacrosanct religious codes become outdated and, though inviolable, require interpretation to make them conform to the times. In the age of Jesus, Pharisees of varying degrees of strictness performed this service. In modern Japan, certain groups, much like the Pharisees of old, busily interpret the constitution while loudly attacking the unconstitutionality of the behavior of all opposing groups. Their wranglings, resembling nothing so much as classical theologians' controversies, have little to do with the cool debates that should accompany legal reform. But this is not surprising, since the constitution they are arguing about is not a legal code but a set of religious commandments.

*8. A Martyr
to Nihonism*

MUCH CAN BE LEARNED ABOUT NIHON-
ism and its adherents from a close perusal of certain of the
classic Japanese writings. Among these I would list the
Kojiki (Record of Ancient Matters) and the *Nihon-Shoki*
(Chronicles of Japan), compiled in 712 and 720 respectively.
Both are official documents, interweaving myth, legend,
and history so as to flatter the reigning dynasty. Next in
chronological order is the great anthology of early poetry
called the *Man'yoshu,* put together at the end of the Nara
Period (646–794), followed by the *Genji Monogatari* (Tale
of Genji), a novel written between 1008 and 1020 by a
court lady-in-waiting named Murasaki Shikibu. At about
the same time, another lady-in-waiting, Sei Shonagon,
wrote *Makura no Soshi* (Pillow Book), a memoir that gives
a clear picture of court life. In the Kamakura Period
(1185–1392), the foremost work is the *Heike Monogatari*

(Tale of the Heike), essentially a collection of war romances of strong emotional appeal to Japanese even today. In the twentieth century the works of such writers as Soseki Natsume and Yasunari Kawabata are classics of Nihonism.

For myself, I have discovered that one work is a satisfactory shortcut to extensive reading. It is called *Hikawa Seiwa* (Reminiscences from Hikawa) and contains numerous anecdotes about important figures involved in the Meiji Restoration (1868). The work is an unexcelled source of material on the Japanese, and not the least of its values is that it was written by one of the outstanding figures of the nineteenth century, Katsu Awa (also called Kaishu Awa).

Katsu was born in 1823 into a household too poor to provide its members with three full meals a day. It was his good fortune to be attached to the court of the Tokugawa shogun Ieyoshi at the age of twelve, thereby being launched on a course of training that led to a career crowded with activity and change. For instance, he was instrumental in organizing a modern navy for the shogunate; he traveled to the United States in an age when very few Japanese ever left the shores of their homeland; he negotiated settlements with the Choshu clan, which was in a state of open rebellion against the shogunate; he carried out negotiations with diplomats of all kinds; and after the shogunate fell in 1868, he was one of its few adherents to survive to play an active part in the Meiji Restoration. Obviously such a man made many enemies, yet it is said that he never called on the services of personal guards and never even wore the two swords to which he was entitled by rank. For the ordinary mortal, simply analyzing and dealing with current problems is a full-time job, but Katsu went beyond the present to make forecasts about the future and to take steps in accordance with his estimation of things to come. He is a classic example of what I mean by the political genius of the Japanese; and all foreigners who are even slightly knowledgeable about the Japan of his time agree in his praises.

Outstanding and successful, Katsu was known to have been an acute observer of human nature and a caustic commentator on what he saw. For example, after having returned from the United States, he was interviewed by a councilor to the shogun. He describes the interview in this way: "After I returned from the United States, the councilor to the shogun said to me: 'You are now a man of some discernment; at any rate, you have been abroad. Tell me, while there, did anything especially catch your eye? Tell me all about it.' I replied that peoples' actions are much the same past or present, East or West, and that I had noticed nothing very different in America. The councilor came back with: 'That cannot be. You must have noticed something different.' I then said that if I had any observation to make it was this: in America people in high places, whether in private or public life, are all very clever; in this they differ sharply from us. At this the councilor's eyes widened in surprise. After scolding me roundly, he exclaimed: 'Remove this insolent fool!'"

Worldy, sharp-tongued, and successful as he was, Katsu held two of his contemporaries in great respect: one was the Confucian scholar Yokoi Shonan and the other was the man whom I have called a martyr to Nihonism, Saigo Takamori, one of the leading military men of his age. Saigo's career, some of which is related by Katsu, tells a good deal about Nihonism and its effect upon Japanese.

Born in 1827 into a lowly samurai family connected with the Satsuma clan, one of the major clans in Kyushu, Saigo became a staff officer in the shogunal army, and before the downfall of the Tokugawas was instrumental in putting down a rebellion engineered by the powerful Choshu clan. Later, however, when Satsuma and Choshu cooperated to overthrow the shogunate, Saigo was one of the chief military leaders of the forces that, after effecting what was called a restoration of imperial power, marched on Edo to occupy the castle there. Though he participated actively in the first stages of the establishment of the Meiji government, Saigo's sympathies remained those of a conservative samurai. Consequently, as he saw the older feudal order being razed to make way for a new kind of Japan, he became displeased and finally resigned from the government and returned to Satsuma. There he became the center of a group of samurai reluctant to allow all the old ways to pass. In the end, these men formed an army, under Saigo's not entirely enthusiastic leadership, and rebelled against the government that Saigo had been helpful in establishing. The Saigo troops mobilized, but they were no match for the much superior government conscription army led by Yamagata Aritomo. In September of 1877, after bloody fighting, Saigo and his army met defeat and destruction. Saigo was wounded and, at his own request, was beheaded on the battlefield by a close friend.

In spite of the feeling Katsu had for Saigo, most of the anecdotes he relates about the man are too pallid to convey to the Western reader the source of the great reverence the worldly, intelligent, and successful politician felt for the military leader. For example, when Saigo and six members of the imperial committee entered Edo Castle in token of assuming the reins of power in the name of the emperor, all was not as placid as surface conditions seemed to suggest. Many of the old shogunal retainers had blood and assassination on their minds. Katsu himself admits to having entertained thoughts of violence. As the imperial delegation entered the castle, the atmosphere was so alive with flashes and forebodings of danger that one of Saigo's men became muddled to the extent that he proceeded, against custom, to enter a building without having removed both sandals. Saigo, however, was unperturbed. After arriving in the place appointed for him, he sat, dozed briefly, awakened, and once again slept, this time soundly. In relating this story Katsu shows little more than Saigo's great calm and self-possession, but his tone is of the greatest reverence. In another instance, however, one senses this admiration of Saigo to a much greater extent.

Before his entry into Edo Castle, Saigo held brief negotiations with Katsu, as shogunal representative, in Shinagawa, not far from Edo. Katsu describes these "negotiations" in a very strange way. In fact, the talks can hardly be called true mutual negotiations, for Katsu, making the sole exception of his unwillingness to hold a certain princess as hostage, left all other matters totally to Saigo's discretion. Saigo, for his part, claiming ignorance of the state of affairs in Edo, said that he relied on Katsu to make all arrangements. Nowhere in this exchange as reported is it possible to catch a glimpse of the shrewd Katsu who had earlier skillfully manipulated English diplomats and who had wheedled the Russians into evacuating the island of Tsushima in the straits between Kyushu and Korea. Clearly Katsu regarded Saigo as something apart from the usual run of mortals, but what is the reason for this attitude?

I think we can find a key in a remark made by Katsu to the effect that only a man of Saigo's moral stature could truly understand Saigo. Katsu intimates that Saigo, neither a politician nor a government official, is basically a man of noble mind and thus incomprehensible to the worldly. I think he is describing a person very like the great Jewish rabbis or the Christian saints. Saints are often recluses—Saigo himself was one—but they must also sometimes possess the attributes of men of political affairs. St. Francis of Assisi, one of the most outstanding Christian saints, may or may not have lived in the wilderness and talked with the birds. But it is a fact that he was politically active enough—in modern terms—to follow the Crusaders to Egypt and to try to proselytize the Muslims. St. Bernard, too, crossed the Alps on several occasions for the sake of political negotiations. In Christian terms, a saint is an embodiment of the Christian ideal, a man devoid of self. Since all of the actions of a saint are open and clear, he enjoys universal confidence. No matter that his costume is a coarse gown with rope belt, no matter that he begs for food or that he walks barefoot wherever he goes, he is welcome at all gates. He may express his opinions openly, and when matters degenerate to dispute, he plays the role of arbitrator.

In terms of Nihonism Saigo Takamori fits this definition of a saint, as Katsu's attitude toward him makes clear. Had Katsu thought he was negotiating with a staff officer of the imperial forces, it is unlikely that he would

have immediately conceded all things without some resistance. After all, had he not shown his acumen and skill
at outwitting diplomats on numerous occasions? He left
everything to the discretion of Saigo because he knew
in his heart that this saint would act in complete accordance with the basic philosophy, laws, and commandments of Nihonism. Saigo, too, recognizing in Katsu a
man who thoroughly understood the precepts of their
common religion, was willing to leave all concrete arrangements to him. Just as Christian saints received full
powers of arbitration in medieval disputes, so Saigo accepted the commission to carry out the transfer of Edo
Castle, not in the spirit of a military undertaking but in
that of a religious task. In agreeing to perform this operation he was in effect saying: "Though there will be many
difficult disputes, I accept the responsibility and dedicate
my whole self to fulfilling this duty." This is not the attitude of an imperial staff officer, but that of a follower
of Nihonism who intends to make all decisions in accordance with his beliefs.

I have said that Saigo is a martyr of Nihonism. Having
now shown the saintliness of his nature, I shall go on to
discuss his martyrdom. Though defeated in battle against
the government, Saigo later became a great popular hero.
There is a large bronze statue of him in Ueno Park, the
scene of fighting during the seizure of Edo by the imperial forces; and a shrine has been dedicated to his mem-
ory. The Japanese veneration of Saigo resembles nothing
so much as placing a halo behind the head of a martyred
saint.

There are various kinds of martyrdom. Saigo's belongs
to the category in which conditions press in on an in-

dividual and make martyrdom the only way out of a situation. Katsu says in the *Hikawa Seiwa:* "[Saigo's] passing cannot be understood by the worldly mortal. . . . It was as if an urge pursued him until, unless he took some action, the situation would become intolerable." Comparing his own philosophy with that of the man he considered a saint of the faith, Katsu goes on to say: "If Saigo had not had the kind of adherents he had, things would not have turned out as they did. I have no adherents; for that reason I am alive today and have come far enough in the world to have been made a nobleman. But, if I had had as many followers as Saigo, I too would have been forced to do something for their sakes. But I lack the goodness to enter into a suicide pact. I would have chosen some other way." Indeed, Katsu probably would have done otherwise, but for Saigo, the saint and the personification of the ideal of Nihonism, there was no other way. His death was a classic martyrdom.

There are major and minor martyrs; Saigo was a major one, but Nihonism has minor ones too. For instance, the famous Forty-seven Ronin, samurai who avenged the death of their lord and were consequently ordered to commit ritual hara-kiri, are minor martyrs. Today they are memorialized at a temple in Tokyo called the Sengaku-ji, where smoke continually rising from votive incense does not symbolize, as a certain Englishman once remarked, the Japanese devotion to revenge. Not all people who have exacted vengeance are regarded by the Japanese as martyrs. The Forty-seven Ronin attained this degree of veneration because their actions were in accordance with the rules, precepts, and laws of Nihonism. Because they followed the dictates of their beliefs, these men died. They are therefore martyrs to the faith. It is scarcely to be wondered then that incense continues today to rise in their honor at the Sengaku-ji. As I have said, Saigo is a different case. He was a major martyr because he was a veritable personification of the devotion to humanity that is the central element of Nihonism. In this sense, his life and recorded accounts of his actions are invaluable material for research into the nature of this faith.

Certain of Saigo's writings—notably the *Nanshu Ikun* (Dying Instructions of Saigo Takamori; Nanshu is Saigo's posthumous Buddhist name)—show him to be a religious man instead of a politician. There is nothing of political slogan or motto and certainly no political scheming in the Machiavellian tradition in what Saigo wrote. He dealt with much larger subjects, as this quotation shows: "The Way belongs to the Universe and Nature. People who would follow it must revere heaven. One's aim must be the reverence of heaven. Heaven means to love others and oneself in the same way; that is, in the same spirit. Make heaven, not human beings, your companion. Strive with all your being to make heaven your companion. And, without finding fault with others, seek out your own shortcomings."

And, in commenting upon the concept of *yoju* (i.e., a short life, a long life), Saigo writes:

"The concept of *yoju* means life is both short and long. It is of great importance to everyone from scholar to laborer. Anyone unable to harmonize life and death will fail to understand the principles of heaven. Ordinary people, reluctant to abandon life, hate death because they are unable to stop making a distinction between the two. For this reason, there are many selfish people; they do not learn the teachings of heaven. A person who accurately understands these teachings, however, need give no consideration to life and death. One does not know when one will be born and there is no way of knowing when one must die. For this reason there is no cause to be concerned about or to discuss the question of life and death. Therefore, since in a sense one is not living, one need not make distinctions between life and death. In short, one must clearly understand that life and death are not two things. If one can grasp this idea, one will have entered the realm of the principles of heaven, and all one says and does will agree with those principles. Once the entire being is united with the principles of heaven, one has attained a stage of high morals and ethics. In this state, since there is no death, one must think only in terms of returning the life one received from the universe. It must be returned unaltered. Thus human beings and heaven are one, and the end of life is only a returning to the universe.

"All living things fear death. Human beings upon death become their own spirits. While fearing death, however, we ought to seek a reason not to fear it. Man's thoughts and his body belong to heaven. The right of life and death rests with heaven, and we must accept this truth naturally and obediently. We are not aware of the happiness of living in nature, and we must not be saddened by dying in nature. Heaven brings life into being, and heaven takes life away. We must leave all to heaven; then there will be nothing to fear. Our nature is that of heaven, and our bodies are vessels for heaven. While it is a thing related to the spirit, the body is a chamber for heaven. When the wandering soul is transformed, however, heaven abandons the chamber. Post-death is, in other words, pre-life; and pre-life is post-death. Since the true home of our spirits is outside both life and death, what have we to fear? This is true in day or night, in dark or light, at the beginning and at the end. In all things, know the principle of death and life, and all other things will become simple and clear. We must always examine ourselves on the basis of this principle."

A man imbued with and true to the kind of faith Saigo sets forth here would be able, when the need arose, to die upon the receipt of no more than a single letter. During his last battle, in 1877, Saigo retreated to Mount Shiro. The government forces against whom he was fighting built a stockade to contain Saigo's forces and guarded it carefully. Yamagata, the leader of the government's troops, sent Saigo a letter saying that he felt it would be regrettable to inflict great fatalities and injuries upon Saigo's forces. Upon reading this letter, Saigo resolved to kill himself rather than live and go against Yamagata's desires. Upon receiving word of this, Yamagata said that the death of the bravest general in the nation was a great loss, and he wept for some time.

Realizing that Yamagata was giving him a chance to spare his men when he wrote of the slaughter that would ensue if Saigo and his forces continued their resistance, Saigo sacrificed himself to save others' lives. Compare this martyr's death to the acts of Napoleon, who abandoned his troops in Egypt, led many more to death and destruction in the snowy wastes of Russia, and even after all of this, insisted on holding a virtually nation-breaking conscription for the battle of Leipzig. Primarily neither a politician nor a man of military nature, Saigo would have been unable to do any of those things. But the contrast between the two men extends to attitudes on small matters as well as to momentous events involving many human lives. For instance, while a prisoner on Saint Helena, Napoleon was annoyed because he thought the guards did not treat him in a manner befitting the station of a former emperor. Saigo, on the other hand, considered being a general of the army or a lowly peasant farmer all the same. It is said of him that he once returned to his old mountain home and took up residence in his house in Takemura. He worked in the fields every day and called himself Takemura Kichi. One morning, as he was carrying a bucket of night soil, he met a samurai who had broken the strap on his wooden clog. Calling to Saigo, the samurai demanded that he repair the strap. Saigo meekly did as he was ordered. Some years later Saigo told the story to the same samurai, who was appalled at what he had unwittingly done. Saigo laughingly apologized for having brought the matter up at all.

One can imagine what Napoleon's reaction to a demand to repair a clog strap might have been. In his willingness to do any kind of work, Saigo resembles many saints and rabbis who toiled at menial labor. No work, however humble, diminishes the greatness of a true spiritual leader, but such men can come into being only in a deeply religious society that provides the proper circumstances for their lives, work, martyrdom, and subsequent reevaluation by the people.

Saigo Takamori was, as I have shown, a great leader, a personification of the ideals of Nihonism, and ultimately a martyr to his beliefs, but his martyrdom differed fundamentally from those of the Judeo-Christian tradition. The path leading to Saigo's death was unlike that trod by the first-generation followers of Christ. The Christians believed in eternal life but thought that the universe is finite. In fact they believed the universal end was not too far in the offing; consequently, they considered martyrdom only natural. Saigo, too, felt this way about the martyr's death, but that is where the similarity ends, for he believed that the universe is eternal and that life is finite and must return to the universe, which gave it birth. The special attack forces used during the Pacific War, too, were encouraged and bolstered by the belief that death is no more than a returning to the eternal home. The Christian idea of a finite universe doomed to destruction is incomprehensible to Japanese, who believe the exact opposite.

The idea that the universe is doomed, as expressed by Jesus and Paul, had certain aspects of primitiveness suited to the needs of people living two thousand years ago. Although about a thousand years later, in the time of Maimonides, the philosophy had become more advanced and progressive, it nonetheless still contained the idea of living in a terminal phase. The members of the Christian branch of Nihonism, on the other hand, neither accept the teaching of Jesus and Paul in this way nor live as if the universe were moving toward cataclysm. On the contrary, they interpret Jesus's teachings to mean that human beings, after a short life, return to heaven. For that reason, it is wrong to devote all of one's life forces to the transient world. Since this is the philosophy set forth by Saigo Takamori in one of the passages I quoted earlier, it seems entirely reasonable to assume that a martyr from the Christian branch of Nihonism would follow the path Saigo trod instead of that of the early Christian martyrs.

9. Contractual and Parental Deities

THERE ARE GOOD REASONS BEHIND the fame of the Jews as skillful, cautious handlers of money. Since they have never had a national currency of their own, they have no emotional feelings about any given set of bills and coins. Almost everyone feels a certain pride and security in using the currency of his own nation. On the other hand, while realizing intellectually that any stable currency is as good as it purports to be, people often accept it less readily than their own familiar money. All of this is connected with emotions that the Jews have not experienced because they have never had their own national money. Consequently, they regard marks, francs, pounds, and dollars as purely economic tools and will convert any currency without compunction when it seems to be about to decline in value. This objectivity toward currency often provokes a condemnation of the Jews as unfeeling and heartless when in fact it is the most natural of reactions from a people who regard money pragmatically and who can in fact do without it entirely, as the kibbutzim of Israel show. The injunction against borrowing—though Jews are permitted to lend—in Deuteronomy and the idea that a person will one day be called to account for what he owns inspire the Jews to keep a firm grip on what they have and to refrain from careless spending. This, in the eyes of less closely regulated peoples, looks like stinginess, as does the Jewish tendency to live less well than one's income would permit. But this last derives from the historical tradition of setting apart certain sums for certain things and of not touching them for ordinary purposes. The ancient tithe is probably the source of this approach to financial management. Though the Jews no longer tithe— philanthropy has taken the place of tithing—the giving of one-tenth of an individual's produce was originally a contractual arrangement, and in this sense is symbolic of the entire relation between the Jews and their God.

In an earlier part of this book, in a discussion of the dialectic of Micah, I mentioned God's threat to destroy Israel. Why should the deity of a people become so enraged as to be willing to effect such punishment? The answer to this question is found in the Jewish interpretation of their duty to God under their covenant with Him. The relation between the Jews and God is not that of parent and child—about which I shall speak more in the following pages—but that between adopted child and adoptive parent. Perhaps this sounds strange, but the meaning becomes clear when one recalls that an adoption is a parent-child relation established by contract. The Old Testament says that God selected the Jews to be His people from a number of other peoples and secured them to Himself through a covenant. This is the origin of the Jewish philosophy of the Chosen People, which does not indicate, as the Japanese sometimes mistakenly interpret it, a sense of being an elite. Ultimately, in the light of this arrangement, God is the adoptive and the Jews the adopted party. But this whole concept is most distasteful to the Japanese, who feel that a relationship of this kind between a divinity and a people is abnormal. I shall talk more of the Japanese attitude, but here I want to sketch in the historical background supporting the Jewish belief that such a relationship is neither new nor odd.

Historians and theologians probably advance a number of profound reasons for the Jewish attitude, but in essence it is very simple to explain. It all springs from the experiences of Moses, who was all his life a kind of adopted child. Abandoned by his mother, who sought to circumvent the Pharaoh's edict that male Hebrew children were to be killed, and taken into the household of the Pharaoh's daughter, he did not fully realize what he was until the day he slew an Egyptian who was beating a Hebrew. Later, after fleeing into the land of the Midianites, he dwelt in the house of the priest Jethro, whose daughter he married. Many scholars believe that the name of the God of the Israelites, Yahweh (Jehovah), derives from that of Jaha, the god of the Midianites, whose manifestations were the wild winds and the thunder. By marrying into Jethro's house, and in a sense becoming an adopted son of the family, Moses naturally became an adopted son of the god Jaha too. After he returned to Egypt and led the Israelites into the land of the Midianites, Moses climbed Mount

Sinai and there made a contract with the god of the people of Jethro. The second of the Ten Commandments, "Thou shalt have no other gods before me," might very well be interpreted to mean thou shalt have no other father but me. Should this commandment be broken, the contract between the people and God becomes null and void, and Jehovah and His adopted children are no longer related. To honor the covenant with God has meant that for three thousand years the Jews have had to abide by God's laws down to the last jot and tittle—and this sense of duty has extended to all contracts into which Jews have entered.

Jesus and Paul thought in the same basic way. They would not have dreamed of rejecting the covenant and laws of God. They did, on the other hand, assert that blind and absolute obedience to the word of God can lead to disobedience of that word. This is the philosophy of the dialectic of Micah and the principle underlying the concept that the unanimous decision is invalid. This way of thinking was current in the time of Christ, and it is not surprising that he and Paul should have reflected it. Their greatness lies in the ability of their thought to persist after the temporal and spatial philosophic atmosphere that produced it has long since vanished. It is a mistake, however, to consider Christianity as we know it a mirror image of the philosophies of Jesus and Paul. Obviously it is not, because Christianity has been subjected to a large number of outside influences. To give only a single instance, I might point out a debt Christianity owes to Mithraism: Sunday is a Mithraic not a Biblical tradition.

When the Europeans accepted the Oriental religion of Jesus of Nazareth, they too entered into an adopted-adoptive relationship. That is to say, the God of Christianity is related to them by contract. But the members of the Christian branch of Nihonism, though they may from time to time mouth words like "God by contract," are incapable of understanding what this truly means.

Like the Jews, the Japanese were a tribal people in the distant past. Unlike the Jews, they felt a blood and not a contractual relationship with their deities. Blood ties, of the kind existing between mother and child, are eternal. It is true that one can disinherit a child, but such a step is purely social and in no way alters the fact of the relation itself. To the Japanese way of thinking, this and only this is the kind of bond that can exist between a people and their god, whether it be the Sun Goddess Amaterasu or the God of the Israelites. In times of trouble or when the children disobey, the God of the Jews threatens complete destruction. But the Japanese can only understand divine punishment in terms of a chastisement of love. As the parent lion in the Oriental fable can lovingly drop its cub into a valley of a thousand blades in order to teach it how to protect itself, so—believe the Japanese—God only punishes His children to show them how much He loves them. It is only natural then that the Japanese should interpret Paul's teaching to the effect that man shall be saved by faith and not works as indicative of an abolition of the Law in favor of a trusting, innocent, and childish worship. In fact, when Jesus and Paul taught, they had audiences that understood the tradition and background of the covenant and the laws of God, but the members of the Christian branch of Nihonism, convinced that the truth of the scriptures lies in their implications and not in their words, interpret the teachings as something that they manifestly are not. In other words, the Japanese convert the Bible into a classic of Nihonism.

All great traditions and religions have been subject to outside influences, and all of them have adapted the materials they borrowed from other faiths and cultures. Contact with Christianity was a catalytic force in the crystallization of Nihonism. It made possible the use of Christian systems, methods, ways of thinking, and doctrinal expressions. But, in the final analysis, Nihonism is not Christianity. The Japanese are themselves well aware of this, and they often speak of the Japanese interpretation of the Bible and of a Japanese grasp of Christianity. This of course does not imply that they do not understand the Bible at all but that they understand it in their own way. Nor is this odd. For instance, an American will find meanings in Zen concepts that a Japanese will not, just as a Japanese will give a different meaning to, say, divine punishment than a Westerner would. Even at that, those Nihonists who have come into contact with Christianity understand their own religion best.

A naive idea grew up in the Meiji era that modern Nihonism was a blend of the way of the samurai and the way of the Christians. In this interpretation the writings of Mencius are the Japanese Old Testament and those of Christianity its New Testament. This view is not tenable, however, for the fact is that Japanese commentaries on the New Testament are influenced by the belief, discussed in Chapter Six, that all judgments must be based on a sense of humanity and not upon inflexible precepts derived from non-human abstractions. I have already noted that this belief is of central importance to Nihonism, and I must add here that I know of no Japanese who discuss the New Testament without reference to it. The most striking example of these contrasting elements is of course Jesus's confrontation with the Pharisees. In this instance the Japanese consider Christ the very epitome of love and humanity and the Pharisees corrupt, inhuman legalists. Although there may be some doubt as to whether the issue between the two was quite so clear-cut as this, the Japanese entertain none.

The teachings of Paul about the saving effects of faith have had a most stimulating effect on the members of Nihonism. But their interpretation of it varies from the standard Christian idea. It is worthwhile at this point to go into the Japanese interpretation a little more deeply, since it reveals some interesting facets of their approach to religion. The Japanese think Paul's doctrine means that faith alone is all that is absolutely necessary to salvation. The same feeling is reflected in the instructions Shinto priests give those vis tors to the Meiji Shrine in Tokyo who are inexperienced in the proper ritual. The priest always tells them to be calm because all they must do is to pray innocently and without thinking. Japanese interpret Paul in exactly the same way, though the concept might have surprised him. They believe that in order to worship God one must do no more than be human, innocent, and unself-conscious in worship. In short, one must prostrate oneself voluntarily before God. But such prostration must be clean and disinterested. To introduce into the worship of God a contract—like the idea of obligatory payment of the tithe—sullies religion in their eyes and casts over it an unpleasant tint of profit seeking. Whereas Jews regard their relationship with God as one of covenant and mutual agreement, Japanese think of it only in terms of the eternal bond existing between parent and child.

10. Peoples Without Virgin Births

THOUGH IN ITSELF A FASCINATING subject, upon investigation virgin birth turns out to be less unusual than might be imagined. For example, someone who is fond of such research has estimated that on the Eurasian continent recorded instances of virgin births amount to some 856 cases. The numbers of unrecorded instances would probably swell the sum to enormous size. Some famous figures said to have been born of virgins are the founder of the Ch'ing (Manchu) dynasty in China, the Greek philosopher Plato, and of course Jesus of Nazareth. Two of the world's peoples, however, have never experienced this particular miracle: they are the Japanese and the Jews. It is true that in discussing the Japanese I must admit that my knowledge is limited. There may have been Japanese virgin births of which I am ignorant, but as far as I have been able to find out, at no time since the age of the myths, when the brother and sister Izanami and Izanagi brought forth the Japanese islands, has a Japanese laid claim to virgin birth; and certainly no one has been afforded special treatment and dignity because of such a legend. When I turn to the case of the Jews, because of the single outstanding instance of Jesus I may seem to be in error in denying the existence of any Jewish tale of virgin birth, but as I shall show, my grounds are firmer than might appear at first glance.

To clarify this point I need to examine briefly the true historical background and nature of the Gospels of the New Testament. Aside from some few parts appended at a later date, the New Testament is not a Christian writing but a group of texts written by Jews living in what I shall call the New Testament Age. There is a gap of at least three centuries between the writing of this set of books and the formation of Christianity as an organized religion. The Jews from the time of Moses lived under the laws of and in covenant with one almighty God and never embraced the idea of a divine trinity. Certainly the crucifixion of a divine figure never entered their minds. In short, the relationship between Christianity and the Bible has always been one-sided; that is to say, Christianity has depended on the Bible, but the Bible has never truly needed Christianity. In fact, until the Council of Nicaea (A.D. 325) disputes and intellectual battles that would be difficult for the modern mind to comprehend raged around attempts to incorporate the idea of Christ's divinity into the New Testament.

This slight digression has been made to establish quite firmly the fact that the New Testament is largely a Jewish work written for the Jews during the New Testament Age.

But in asserting this, have I disproved my earlier statement that the Jews lack a tradition of virgin birth? To answer this, I shall examine the evidence to discover whether this legend can in fact be attributed to the Jews.

The Gospel according to Mark is not only the oldest of the first four books of the New Testament, it is also the one on which the other three are based. In it there is nothing about the virgin birth or even about the childhood of Jesus. Mark does, however, clearly say that when Jesus began preaching his mother, Mary, was extremely surprised. No doubt thinking that he must have gone mad, she and her other children set out to bring Jesus home. This seems to suggest that both his birth and early youth had been completely ordinary, since his mother would scarcely have been so shocked by his preaching if she had already experienced the Annunciation and the Nativity complete with celebrating angels. I might mention in passing that although Mark says that Christ's grave was found empty he says nothing (except in some later additions to the text) about anyone's having met or spoken with Christ after the Resurrection. John, too, is silent on the topic of the virgin birth and even tacitly denies that Bethlehem was the scene of the Nativity. Indeed, the subject in general is irrelevant to John's message.

The idea of virginity as found in the Gospel of Matthew may well be the result of a linguistic error. His reason for bringing up the point is to prove that a prophecy made by Isaiah has been fulfilled in Christ. The famous passage— "Behold, a virgin shall conceive, and bear a son, and his name shall be called Emmanuel"—would have been familiar to all Jews of his time. It is true that the Hebrew word used in the text to describe the person who shall bear a son means young woman and not virgin. But in the New Testament Age, Jews spoke either Aramaic or Greek and not Hebrew. Furthermore, Matthew was probably quoting from the Septuagint, the oldest Greek version of the Old Testament, prepared in Alexandria in the third and second centuries B.C. In this translation, the Hebrew word for young woman in Isaiah is rendered by means of the Greek word *partenos,* which does in fact mean virgin. This may have been an error, or it may have been that at the time the Septuagint was translated partenos meant a young woman and not necessarily a virgin. Not being a Greek scholar, I cannot say which is true, but since the same word may be used in different senses according to time and place, the second explanation seems the likely one. Whatever the truth of the matter, however, Matthew, in recalling the words of Isaiah, was stressing the fulfillment of the prophecy that a Messiah would come and not the virginity of the mother of Jesus.

The Gospel of Luke is an entirely different matter. This man, called the first Catholic, originated the legend of the virgin birth and all the other elements so often dramatized in Christmas pageants, including the Annunciation and the rejoicing of the angelic hosts. As a matter of fact, from a Jewish standpoint, Luke and his writings are totally foreign. This is not surprising, for Luke was a Greek born in Antioch and a member of a reformed branch of Judaism. His work is Greek in feeling and redolent of the tone of the Greek mystery religions. Furthermore, he was not writing for the Jews; his intended audience was a Roman named Theophilus, who is thought to have been a high official. In short, instead of being a Jew writing for other Jews, Luke is a Greek addressing a Roman and dealing with a Jesus that he has carefully removed from his Judaic setting. Luke's work, as might be expected, most aptly fits the needs of Christian believers. He never met either Jesus or Paul—who never met Jesus, either, for that matter—and his Gospel and the Acts of the Apostles are, in the final analysis, compilations of carefully selected material, which Luke brought into line with his own interpretations. As if to underscore the non-Jewish nature of his writings, Luke vehemently denies any connection between Jesus and the Old Testament (that is, with the Jews). There is no denying the superior quality of Luke's writing and the beauty of his Greek. Markion, an early Church father and so-called heretic, went so far as to say that the writings of Luke and Paul are the only parts of the Bible worth keeping. Certainly Luke established the Christian image of Jesus and in doing so severed the ties between Christianity and Judaism.

Aside from some unique elements, however, the teachings of Christ himself are not widely at variance with those of his rabbi contemporaries. As many scholars insist, there were pre-Christian Jewish sects whose doctrines shared elements with those of Christianity. One of these groups was the Essenes, who wrote the Dead Sea Scrolls. Dr. Matthew Black, an authority on the New Testament, has analyzed these writings and explained their connections with Christian philosophy.

Two very important points in Christian theology, however, have made it completely unacceptable to the Jews. One is the virgin birth and the other is the idea of Christ as king and priest, descended from the house of David, and the Son of God. Being born of a virgin, by its very miraculous nature, bestows on Christ a special dignity that Jewish leaders have never had. Throughout the history of Judaism, its great men have been born in a perfectly ordinary fashion, and their positions and fame derived not from their background but from being chosen by God to perform certain roles and proceeding to fulfill them in an outstanding way. Moses was an abandoned child, Samuel was the son of a second wife, David was the youngest child of a village headman, and Elijah's antecedents are not even known. Singled out by God to do a task, these men seldom enjoyed happiness as a result of their exalted positions. Indeed, Moses himself, sensing the weight of the burden God called on him to bear, attempted to escape his duty but could not. Nor were the lofty ranks of these men ever hereditary, as kingship often is. Each of them was selected by God, and only people thus chosen could ever attain to these high stations. Monarchy is out of harmony with the structure of Judaism, though it is true that from the time of Saul to that of Zedekiah Israel was a kingdom. (Incidentally, in the case of the latter, it would be more accurate to say that Joachim was king and Zedekiah regent.) Fundamentally, the Jews—like most desert people—believe that all men are equal under one God and that birth in itself does not convey distinction. Obviously such people reject the Christian assertions that Jesus of Nazareth was the Son of God (a God who is a far cry from the mighty deity of Genesis who created the entire universe and everything in it, including death) and that descended from David (the genealogy is false) he is both priest and King.

I do not assert that the Jews are without tales of marvelous beings, which are found in the traditions of all peoples. There is a certain amount of this kind of thing in the Book of Genesis and in a document written during the time of Christ and found among the Dead Sea Scrolls. In none of the Jewish tales of supernatural beings, however, does virgin birth play a role and in none of them are the mysterious creatures themselves considered in any way great; they are only weird. A people who treat the supernatural in such a way must inevitably reject the notions that Jesus is to be revered because of the conditions surrounding his birth and that he is the Son of God. Consequently, the Jews lack, as do the Japanese, the virgin-birth tradition.

The reasons on the Japanese side, which are entirely different, begin with the question of direct lineal descent. In a nation claiming an unbroken line of descent from the mythological gods and goddesses, not only for the ruling house but also for all the people, lineage occupies a place of paramount importance. One of the aspects of Japanese life that fascinates other peoples is the persistence even today of the tradition of natural or chosen successors, which extends into all fields including politics, economics, art, performing arts, and religion. The idea of the *iemoto,* the person who stands as the head of a school of, say, Ikebana or the tea ceremony, permeates everything in Japan. No matter if the person who succeeds the iemoto is a true offspring, an adopted child, or a disciple, the important thing is that the line of descent be maintained. In some cases, students may break away from the parent school, but even then, in one way or another—for example by using the name of the parent school in that of their own institution—they invariably strive to assert a relation to the original group. The imperial house of Japan claims unbroken descent from the mythological age. Since this heritage is of the greatest importance, a virgin birth somewhere along the line would upset the whole system. Such a thing is therefore unthinkable. There is no place in the Japanese system for a genealogy of the kind provided for Jesus by Luke. But, whereas the Jewish reason for rejecting virgin birth is the belief that all great things occur as a result of God's commandments, the Japanese consider virgin birth out of the question because it would represent a break in the all-important lineage.

A second reason for the Japanese lack of a virgin-birth tradition is to be found in their attitude toward sex and procreation. Japanese Bible scholar Zenta Watanabe has said that the Old Testament regards procreation as good and the sex act as sinful. Although to the eyes of the Japanese the Bible's teaching might look this way, in fact it is somewhat different. Peoples of the nomadic tradition naturally think of breeding and raising domestic animals as profitable. Even when the domestic animals in question are slaves, the same idea holds true: keeping female slaves pregnant as often as possible means maximum profit, since the children born of those slaves are concrete economic assets. To the nomadic way of thinking, sex is neither clean nor unclean: it is an essential part of life and business. It must not, however, become an object of emotional attachment, and the children resulting from the sex act are neither pledges of love nor treasures capable of being increased. In short, as profit is sensible and good but miserliness and the cherishing of money for its own sake are bad, so sex and procreation are good, but entangling them in emotional associations is bad.   In a sense this is not unlike the attitude behind the words of warning delivered to the women of the old Japanese pleasure quarters: falling in love is not part of the business. Sex to nomads is an everyday thing, as plowing a field is to farmers; consequently, it is not and it must not become mystical. Interestingly enough, words used to describe the tilling of the soil by nomads who also engage in agriculture are those employed in explaining the sex act.

The Japanese have always regarded sex as anything but run-of-the-mill. In their eyes, it is mystical, romantic, and enmeshed in the most elaborate emotional relations. As I have pointed out, the Japanese have no experience of or connection with the nomadic tradition. It is not surprising therefore that their attitude toward sex should be entirely different from that of nomadic peoples. As is amply illustrated in the famous romance *The Tale of Genji,* from the Japanese standpoint there are no limits to the extent to which love, sex, and romance can be graced with emotionalism and mysticism. This has been the way with the Japanese people since the age of the myths, but modern writers too have commented on the same attitude. For instance, the novelist Junnosuke Yoshiyuki remarked that sexual intercourse without emotional exchange is empty, and an elderly scholar once pointed out that sex without love is like a dim and gaping cave. This distinctive romantic and mystic approach to sex captivated many nineteenth-century foreign visitors to Japan. But it is this very emotionalism that makes virgin birth impossible under Japanese circumstances. Indeed, even very long ago, anyone born of a virgin would have been treated as a freak, not a wonder.

Springing from the general aura of romance that surrounds sex is the Japanese conviction that children and parents are an inseparable unit. Poor Japanese families driven to extremities have been known to commit group suicide. The Japanese newspapers sometimes criticize the parents in these cases for taking their children with them in death. The journalists think that this act indicates the parents' belief that children are their property and a failure to recognize the individual rights of the young. I, however, feel that the writers who express such opinions are in error, for if the parents truly thought of their children as property they might take other steps. I can make my point clear by illustrating the sharply contrasting attitude of people who *do* regard their offspring as expendable commodities. Let us take as an example the case of a typical owner of a slave-worked plantation in the southern United States before the Civil War and the abolition of slavery. This man would have regarded as his property in the fullest sense of the word those children he sired on his slave women. If his financial condition deteriorated severely, he would have had no compunction in putting his young slave son or daughter on the auction block to raise money. Neither the rights nor the feelings of the child would have been of concern to the owner-father, nor would he have ever considered mass suicide, much less his own, because he had money problems. In short, unless parents and children are thought of as a unity subject to one fate, family suicide is out of the question. The idea of the unity of the family rises from the Japanese belief in the mysticism and emotionalism of sex.

Luke was an evangelist of genius without whom Christianity might never have been established. The success of his work can be judged from the fact that the virgin birth he provided for Christ is known in Japan even by people who know nothing else of Christianity. Unfortunately, however, the virgin birth, even when explained as no more than a legend, finds no soil in which to take root in Japan. At the Meiji Restoration, when Japan embarked on a period of strenuous modernization, as is known, she accepted neither technological nor economic assistance from any country. But Christian missionaries did flood through the recently opened doors to the nation. After a century, Christianity has been nationalized; that is, it has been absorbed into Nihonism. The first thing the Japanese eliminated (essentially) from the Scriptures was the virgin birth, unacceptable even as a legend. God will probably be the next to go.

11. Persecution in the Offing

I ALWAYS TELL FELLOW JEWS THAT they must not make remarks like: "Since we are a persecuted people, we have a right to make pronouncements to the rest of humanity." The Japanese too feel entitled to make a similar a statement: "Since we are the only people ever to have suffered an atomic-bomb attack, we have a right to make pronouncements to the rest of mankind." As a Jew, I am within my rights to say that Jews ought not to feel this way. On the other hand, since only a Japanese is truly qualified to admonish the Japanese in such a vein, I must hold my tongue.

The Jews are not the only people in the world ever to have suffered persecution. A list would be long, but for the sake of this discussion, I will consider only the Arabs in Black Africa and the Chinese in Indonesia, both of whom have been victims of severe persecution in recent years.

Although the Japanese press reported little on the plight of the Arabs, newspapers were full of articles about the harassment and deaths of Chinese in Indonesia. Estimates of the number of persons killed ran from two hundred to five hundred thousand. The scale of this bloodshed is horrifying when one considers that some of the world's groups contain no more than half a million members. Just as the victimized Arabs got little space in Japanese newspapers, so the massacres of the Chinese were not emphasized in the news media of the West. Oddly enough, though well informed on the matter, most Japanese barely raised their eyebrows at the horrors perpetrated on the Chinese. Yet the Japanese consider the Chinese a kindred people. On the other hand, when nuclear experiments take place, even if guaranteed harmless to man and animals, almost all Japanese speak out with a single voice of opposition. In contrast, the Jews, who are sensitive to reports of persecution, are much less concerned about nuclear tests. Nor is this surprising. There is a great difference between Hiroshima and Auschwitz. Furthermore, the historical experiences of the two peoples are not the same. There is no doubt that even the remotest chance of another atomic bomb being dropped on Japan would galvanize the nation into a united front of protest. But if I were to warn my Japanese friends that they might someday face persecution by others, I suspect that they would show no reaction at all. The idea simply would not mean anything to them. For that reason it is possibly futile for me to say what I shall say in the following few pages, but since I was born and raised in Japan, I feel that I must speak, even if I am laughed at for my pains.

What happened to the Chinese in Indonesia is an example of a classic pattern of persecution that has occurred again and again in the history of the world. A ruling foreign group (the Dutch in Indonesia) allows another foreign group (the Chinese who had immigrated to Indonesia) to gain significant power in the economic life of a country to the detriment of the native population. When the foreign rulers leave, their native successors at first let matters stand as they were, but eventually nationalism becomes so strong that groups favored in the old days—especially economic middlemen—come under attack. When the Dutch ruled Indonesia, the Chinese enjoyed a favored status, and they rather than the European rulers were the ones who dealt most directly with the native populations. After the collapse of Dutch rule, President Sukarno and his associates—no matter what slogans they devised—did no more than grasp for themselves the power the Dutch had held. They simply moved into the chair the Dutch had occupied, and the Chinese and native Indonesians in no way altered their social positions. It was not until the reign of Sukarno came to a sudden end that large-scale persecutions of the Chinese began. Although the prophecy is grim, I fear that the Vietnamese in Cambodia or the Indians in Black Africa may be among the next groups to face a similar kind of terror.

The history of the Jews provides countless examples of the classic pattern of persecution: one of the oldest is that of the Jewish settlement in Alexandria. Alexander the Great had high regard for the Jews, and when he established Alexandria he afforded them the same rights that he conferred on the Macedonians and Greeks. As matters developed, the Greeks controlled the political life of the city while the Jews became important as economic middlemen. An impressive physical manifestation of the Jews' success was the various buildings *(diplostoön)* constructed by their craft guilds. These buildings, designed on basilicalike plans, were handsome enough to inspire one Rabbi Judah to say: "Whoever has not seen the diplostoön in Alexandria in Egypt has never in his life seen Israel's glory." When the Greek rulers fell, the Jews suffered as did the Chinese in Indonesia centuries later—the diplostoön were destroyed and the blood of many Jews flowed in the streets. Incidentally, it is interesting to notice that this took place before the Christian era: persecution of the Jews did not wait for the appearance of Christians on the stage of history.

The same story was repeated over and over. For instance, when the Moors invaded Spain, the Jews stood between them and the native Spaniards. So great did the economic strength of these Jews grow that their wealth was compared with that of the caliph himself. But fate overtook them as it had the Jews of Alexandria.

Somewhat similar social circumstances once existed in Japan in the Middle Ages. At that time the rice merchants, sakè merchants, pawnbrokers, and other rich groups were the object of numerous so-called "smashings," when poor people broke into their homes, killed, and looted. But the resemblance between the smashings and the experiences of the Jews is only superficial. Both the raiders and their victims were Japanese. In addition, the government simultaneously attempted to suppress the smashings and to rescue the victims. In some cases, statesmen accepted responsibility for the incidents. For example, feudal lords were punished, cabinets resigned in a body, or official money was used to establish relief organizations. In other words, the Japanese applied their special political genius to control the situation.

The methods used to control matters in nations in which the Jews—or the Indonesia Chinese—have been the victims were of an entirely different order. In these instances, governments attempted to overcome crises by turning a native people's dissatisfaction against a non-native scapegoat. Either not seeing or pretending not to see, they allowed the turmoil to rage until the people grew too tired to torment the scapegoat further. Neither the Jews nor the Chinese could do anything about their plight. For two thousand years, the Jews have known all too well what this means; for that reason they are aware of the high cost of security and of the need to take constant steps to ensure it. Unfortunately, however, this very awareness sets up a vicious cycle in which lack of self-confidence becomes suspicion of others (well founded, to be sure, from the standpoint of people submitted to frequent persecution), and this in its turn breeds discrimination and ill feeling in the suspected and thus creates grounds for insane persecution when something untoward occurs.

Since the Japanese have never experienced this cycle, they are incapable of displaying the attitudes that set it into motion. It is true that Japanese immigrants in the United States underwent painful experiences during World War II. But their very hardships have been one of the causative elements in the establishment of a position within American society that is in some ways as secure as that of American Jews.

In the preceding paragraphs I have discussed a classic pattern of persecution and some of its causes. The ones described are not, of course, all the causes. For example, undeniably, certain animosities are stimulated by something that acts on human beings the way odors do. That is to say, the human being is susceptible to dislikes caused by the so-called smells of foreigners, just as a whiff of an approaching strange animal causes a dog to bare his teeth in suspicion and anger. Of course the ill feeling aroused by moods expressed as smells—for instance the imagined garlic odor of the Korean or the Italian, or the general "butter smell" the Japanese sense in all things and people Western —cannot be understood in terms of reason or theory. It is odd (or perhaps totally to be expected) that most peoples use words connected with odor to express feelings of evil associated with the alien, when of course the true causes of suspicion have little or nothing to do with odors. For instance, the Koreans in Japan are supposed to smell of garlic, which is used in many of their pickles and other foods. The fact is that, in a city where Korean food is as popular as it is in Tokyo, to claim to be able to distinguish a Korean from a Japanese by the smell of garlic is patent nonsense. Judging from physical traits it is often impossible to tell a Japanese and a Korean apart, at any rate for a Westerner like me. Nevertheless, a few years ago, not long after a famous incident involving a Korean man named Kim, who, when pursued by the police for a crime, locked himself in a small room and threatened to shoot all who came near, I had an amusing encounter with a Tokyo taxi driver. This driver, claiming to be afraid that any Korean he picked up might blast a hole in the back of his head with a rifle in the fashion of a Mr. Kim, announced to me as I was riding in his vehicle that under no circumstances would he accept a customer of that nationality. I asked him how he was going to tell whether a person standing at the road- side and waving for a cab was or was not Korean. He re- plied that the smell would give the Korean away. To my objection that the only possibility of discerning the telltale odor would occur after a passenger was already in the car with doors shut, the driver returned: "Oh well, if you're going to talk about theories, maybe odor's not the word. It's, you know, a feeling." The same kind of incident could take place anywhere because in human discrimination there is always an animal element that seems to be impossible to describe without the use of words connected with the olfactory sense. All persecution includes this kind of thing, though the extent to which it is a causative factor varies. An extremely enlightening case of this was the massacre of Koreans shortly after the Great Kanto Earthquake of 1923.

According to my classic pattern of persecution there was absolutely no reason for these massacres. At that time a group of Western capitalists were strongly entrenched economically in Japan, and the Koreans by no means occupied a profitable position between them and the Japanese. On the contrary, many Koreans lived and worked under the worst conditions and performed the meanest tasks. In all likelihood, if the Kanto earthquake had not suddenly and devastatingly struck the country, the hideous killings would never have occurred. At any rate, the massacres of the Koreans were not an instance in which a dissatisfied and distressed people use natural disaster as an excuse for taking out their dissatisfaction on a scapegoat. This is clear from the fact that in the almost fifty years that have passed since the earthquake no similar incident and no incident that might even be thought similar has taken place.

No matter who attempts to explain the Korean killings, the true causes are difficult to locate. Intellectual Japanese have attempted to fit the incident into an ideological frame, but I do not believe it will lend itself to such treatment.

Since quite naturally the Koreans cannot talk about it without bitterness and resentment, they are unable to plumb the true reasons. Furthermore, my theory of the social position of the persecuted does not agree with the case. I have said that the likelihood of persecution increases in certain social positions. Peoples who fall victim to persecution may occupy that position, may be related to people occupying that position, or may be mistaken for people in either of these two categories. The Koreans who were brutally slaughtered after the Great Kanto Earthquake, however, were totally unconnected with the social position I describe. Consequently, there are no records of pillage and looting of the kind that frequently took place in the ghettos of the Jews. And to the limits of my ability to investigate, no such acts were in fact perpetrated. From this evidence, I conclude that the persecution of the Koreans was totally animal. Do not mistake my meaning; I am not implying that the Japanese are more animalistic than any other people. In fact there is an element of the animal in all persecution no matter where it takes place. But in Japan the animal cause—the odor of the alien of which I spoke earlier—is the only cause. For that reason, a factor that is difficult to discern in other cases comes clearly to the foreground in persecution in Japan.

In all of the confusion surrounding the massacre of the Koreans, one thing is certain. The Japanese, who were spurred to action by the earthquake and the subsequent cataclysm, sincerely believed that the Koreans in the city had risen up and were about to attack them. I think this is true because a man like Kanzo Uchimura—Christian, antiwar philosopher, and pacifist, who had lived abroad, had a fine education, and was a publisher of books in the

English language—was sufficiently frightened of marauding Koreans that he patrolled his home armed with a wooden sword, his only weapon, which he intended to use to the best of his ability in protecting his family. Certainly if a man of a high intellectual level believed that the Koreans were a menace, it is not surprising that the general populace succumbed to similar suspicions. But why? I do not believe that anyone maliciously circulated inflammatory rumors.

The best way to discover the true nature of the situation is to see it through the eyes of a person with no ideological ax to grind. The following eyewitness account by the mother of a Japanese friend of mine is a relatively unbiased interpretation of the Korean massacre.

When the first tremor hit, she was at home with her three children. Dragging them with her she immediately ran into the garden. Later, when the shaking had subsided and it was possible to stand, she took the children to the home of her brother, who lived next door. Next she dashed back to her own house and attempted to telephone her husband. Another sharp quake struck and she was forced to flee the building to save her life. Afterward she continued to try to make contact for about twenty or thirty minutes before she realized that telephone communications were out of the question under the circumstances. As she turned to go back to her brother's house, she saw a wildly disheveled young woman with a child staggering up the alley in back of her garden. The woman was screaming: "It's awful; we are all going to be murdered!" She claimed to have seen the murderers only a few blocks away. The young woman's half-mad ravings and her shocking appearance made a deep, almost magical, impression on my friend's mother, who immediately ran to a nearby thoroughfare. There she

heard that the Koreans who lived in the dry bed of the
Tama River had formed a large band and were preparing
to attack the Japanese. The more she heard, the more horrendous the tale became: the Koreans were breaking into
and pillaging every house they came across; they were setting fire to homes, throwing poison into wells, and slaying
women and children with scythes. Everyone was convinced
that the only way to safety was to seek asylum in the military barracks. My friend's mother said: "At first I only
half believed what they were saying. But then I thought
that if the telephone office was out of operation, the police
must be paralyzed too. And if that was the case, there was
no one to protect us. What's more, I couldn't forget that
screaming woman in the back of my garden. So, tying one
of my children to my back and taking the other two by
their hands, I set out for the barracks. But before I left I
wrote on the door in big letters: 'We are all safe; have gone
to the military barracks.'"

The reaction of my friend's mother is interesting in connection with my earlier discussion of the Japanese attitude
toward security. Trusting absolutely in the police, they feel
that safety is fully—and without cost—guaranteed by police
protection. When my friend's mother became convinced
that the police were no longer able to operate effectively,
she knew that she must take steps to protect herself and her
family. When asked if she had believed the stories about
the Koreans without reservation, this calm and dignified
lady said:

"I imagine that most of it was true. The Koreans probably did form a large band and begin to move toward safety.
But so did all the Japanese. It's only to be expected that
they should do so. The difference, you see, was that this

mass of Koreans looked different; they wore different clothes and spoke a different language. There was a different feeling about them, and this aroused suspicion.

"At the time, the Koreans were gravel diggers and rubbish collectors. They lived in the bed of the Tama River in board hovels. Mountains of old newspapers and other trash stood everywhere. And they had to cook on small stoves with nothing but kindling and chips of wood for fuel. When the earthquake struck, the whole place must have been burned to the ground in no time. Naturally, the Koreans ran away with nothing but the clothes on their backs.

"The first thing they needed was probably water. So, when they came to a farm with a well, they flocked around it to drink. The Japanese farmer looking on had just gone through the nightmare of the earthquake, and suddenly here was a mob of strange-looking people crowding around his well and jabbering words that he didn't understand. It really isn't surprising that the farmers were alarmed. Even if the Koreans had tried to say something in the way of thanks, fear would have blocked the farmers' ears to their meaning.

"Another thing, in those days farmers took great care of their wells; they even thought of them as holy places. When the Koreans rushed in to drink, the farmers probably thought they were polluting the wells. It may have been that some of the wells were dirtied; I don't know. But I suspect that this was the beginning of the tales of poisoned well water."

The lady's story continues, but I need quote from it no further because everything she said resolves itself into the fact that the Japanese and the Koreans were taking identical steps to save themselves. She even remarked that when they arrived at the military barracks, she and her children became part of a crowd drinking from a well used to water the horses. The fact that the Koreans were butchered for doing no more than the Japanese themselves were doing illustrates an unavoidable aspect of persecution. The black people living in the United States are persecuted for doing things the whites do. They attribute their misfortune to the color of their skin (or to the things it symbolizes). But this is not the case in Japan, as blacks would learn if they visited that country. The skin color of the Koreans and the Japanese is the same. Moreover, there are no exterior physical traits that distinguish one nationality from the other. The secret of the cause of the carnage at the time of the Great Earthquake was an instinctive animal rejection of the alien living in the midst of a homogeneous population.

Returning to the theme of how the position of being a middleman or go-between invites persecution, I would argue that the Japanese today face a serious threat of such persecution. As I noted before, many Japanese may find this ludicrous. Perhaps I am wrong; yet this is what I believe. Economically the world is gradually becoming one unit, within which Japan has come to occupy a place as an important industrial power. Nevertheless, the Japanese are not rulers in the sense that the Alexandrian Greeks or the colonial Dutch or British were. Although the Japanese now produce sophisticated electronic devices, they do not have the great industrial strength to send rockets to the moon, to monopolize military power, or, in short, to shake the world. This kind of strength now rests in the hands of the white Christians and the white Communists. The Japanese, known to the great masses of the non-white peoples of the world for the excellence of their products and services, are in a position similar to that of the Alexandrian Jews. They are honorary white men as the Jews were once, in a sense, honorary Greeks in Alexander's city. Like the reign of the Macedonians and the Greeks, the white Christian-Communist cartel may well weaken and fail. Tokyo, the great diplostoön of the Japanese, is a world criterion for size and splendor, but a wagon sometimes cannot avoid following the tracks of the vehicle that passed before it. For this reason, the Japanese might find an interesting point of reference in the history of the Jews. Of course, today the Japanese, who are more skillful at politics than the Jews, have a strong government and a mighty self-defense force, both of which the Jews of the Alexandrian period lacked, and it is unlikely they will be attacked physically. But other forms of assault may be in the offing.

Some intellectuals hold—and among them are some of the spoiled Japanese children I have already discussed—that Japanese capitalists planned the Korean War for their own profit. Although I do not think this is the whole story, the assertion deserves attention. The Koreans themselves claim that while they were fighting at the thirty-eighth parallel, the Japanese were raking in profits with both hands. In short, they maintain that current Japanese prosperity is built on Korean sacrifices. Whether this is true or false, the Japanese themselves were innocent of underhanded or dishonest dealing in the matter. After World War I, German Jews faced similar criticism. Non-Jewish Germans complained that while they had braved the guns and death of the trenches, the Jews had sat at home in comfort and had made vast fortunes from the war. Undeniably, many Jews were in a position to profit from wartime inflation, but the Kaiser and his military leaders started the war, not the Jews. Nevertheless, it was discontent over Jewish profits during the war that led to Auschwitz.

Many Japanese sincerely believe that one of their nation's main roles is to protect non-white peoples. If we think of the latter as a labor force and white men as management, the Japanese become brilliant intermediaries between the two, a kind of struggle committee. In the years since the end of World War II, the Japanese have come to occupy an important executive rank in world affairs: they are now honorary white men. But if the white managers regard these honorary white men with caution—because of their alien smell—the labor-force peoples too have mixed feelings about them. One reads of restrictions in developing countries aimed at the business activities of Japanese, and the Western press has made much of the concept of the Japanese as economic animals. The Japanese may one day find themselves facing a general hostility that will differ little from that which has inspired persecution of the Jews in many lands. The Japanese middlemen will then be in serious trouble.

12. *Some Misconceptions*

THE JEWS FEEL EXTREMELY CLOSE TO the Japanese, and it is a matter of great joy to them that many Japanese travel to Israel to study. As a matter of fact, aside from the Holy Land itself, the Jews probably have warmer feelings about Japan than about any other country. Unfortunately, however, Japanese journalism often contains a number of mistaken ideas about us, ideas that sound like nothing so much as parroting things picked up from Westerners and Arabs. While trying to make allowances for the differences of opinion that inevitably arise, in the following pages I would like to point out a few of the most glaring misconceptions that the Japanese have about the Jews and their history.

A Japanese would be unable to tolerate a visitor who announced that the stone ramparts around the Imperial

167

Palace in Tokyo are the walls of the castle of the emperor
Jimmu (660–585 B.C.). Similarly, a Jew would have to
laugh if a Japanese said that the Wailing Wall is so named
because it is the place where the Jews cry in mourning over
the lost glory of King Solomon. The worst article written
on the subject by a Japanese contained this ludicrous remark: "The Wailing Wall, a wall from the Temple of
Solomon, is so called because since the time that Jerusalem
was split into Israeli and Jordanian sectors the wall has
been charged with dew, making it seem to weep." It may
well be that someone with a grudge against Israel deliberately sets this kind of rumor afoot. As far as the antiquity
of the custom of gathering at the Wailing Wall is concerned,
the oldest record I have found is of a group of pilgrims from
Bordeaux who reported witnessing such an act in A.D. 333.

The wall is completely unrelated to the temple built by
Solomon. It is part of the extensive reconstruction of the
Temple carried out in 20 B.C. under Herod the Great (37–
4 B.C.). Solomon's Temple was destroyed in 586 B.C. by
the Babylonian king Nebuchadnezzar, although a close
reading of the Bible suggests that the foundations may have
remained. At the same time, leading Jews were carried off
into captivity. After about forty years had passed, however,
Cyrus, the king of the Medes and the Persians, destroyed
the Babylonian power and, taking a course exactly opposite
to that of Nebuchadnezzar, allowed all the captive peoples
to go back to their homelands. A sadly ravaged land greeted
the Jews upon their return. Everything was in ruins, and
the people were downtrodden and disconsolate. Though
the leaders were anxious to rebuild the Temple as a symbol
of the strength of the people, impoverishment and exhaus-
tion gravely complicated their task. Many Jews lacked the

means to rebuild their own dwelling places, and it was of the greatest importance to begin cultivating the land as soon as possible. Such circumstances meant frustration and postponement of the reconstruction of the Temple, but at last under the stimulating encouragement of such prophets as Haggai and Zechariah, after fifty-five years of effort, the Temple was rebuilt. Following this, the city walls were raised again, and when the work was completed, the people rejoiced with a great shout that is said to have echoed over the surrounding plains. As I said, King Herod expanded this Temple, but in the Jewish Wars of A.D. 70, the Romans once again razed it; the so-called Wailing Wall is all that remains today. When we Jews gather there, we recall the indomitable spirit of our forefathers who, among grave trials, succeeded in rebuilding the Temple. The wall is a symbol of our vow to reconstruct our homeland, just as long ago the people, working with one spirit and one desire, recreated the splendid buildings of the Temple. This is definitely not a wall from the glorious Temple of Solomon; it is something more important. It is a symbol of the determination of the Jews, the blood and sweat with which they surmounted overwhelming trials to reconstruct the most important edifice in the land.

Arabs today say that the Jews, having abandoned Palestine two thousand years ago, have now returned, claiming it as their homeland. Some Japanese accept the Arab interpretation, which would deserve support if it were the truth; I myself would be unable to deny it. The problem, however, is whether the Arab claim is based on fact or is only political propaganda. If the latter is the case, there is no need to offer rebuttal, since the aim of political propaganda is not to convince the listener in a rational fashion but to talk loudly enough to drown out the opposition. I shall content myself, therefore, with a simple martialing of historical facts and leave conclusions to the reader.

It is true that during the dispersal following the Jewish Wars of A.D. 70 countless Jews were driven from the land, and today Jews returning there often sigh: "At last to have returned after two thousand years." Certain branches of Jewry have not lived in Palestine for two thousand years; certain others have not dwelt there in three thousand years. But this is not to say that for twenty centuries there have been no Jews in Palestine. There were Jews living there, but having lost their political independence, they became citizens of whatever nation was occupying the country at the time. To claim that for this long period there have been no Jews in Palestine is as senseless as to say that for the more than three decades that Japan controlled the Korean Peninsula there were no Koreans there, since everyone was technically a Japanese citizen.

Herod Agrippa, the last true king of Judea, though in fact a puppet of Rome, had a certain amount of independence because of his alleged assistance in putting Caligula on the Roman throne. At his death, however, Judea came completely under the control of the Roman Empire. The first Jewish revolt against the Romans (I call it a "revolt" because that is the standard Western historical term for the event; in fact it was a war of independence) took place in A.D. 66. The Jewish resistance lasted for four years, but in the end the Romans overcame and destroyed Jerusalem and the Temple. Not discouraged by this, a number of Jews took refuge in Masada, a mountainous fortress on the east shore of the Dead Sea, and committed suicide in A.D.

73 when they could no longer hold out. A second Jewish revolt took place in A.D. 132, but it is not as well documented as the first one, for which we have the detailed accounts in Josephus's *Jewish Wars*. It is clear, however, that Rabbi Akiba was the spiritual leader of the uprising, which was guided in military matters by the pseudo-Messiah Simon Bar-Kochba. For a brief while, Jewish independence was reestablished and currency was issued. Recent excavations have unearthed a letter from Bar-Kochba to one of his subordinates, and it may be that further archaeological research will reveal more details about the second Jewish uprising. It is now known that after three years the Romans completely crushed the revolt. Jews living abroad were forbidden on pain of death to return to their homeland. Later, when Emperor Constantine accepted Christianity, this ban was lifted, and many Jews either returned or made pilgrimages to Palestine.

Under Constantine I, Palestine became important as the Holy Land, the scene of the events in the life of Christ. Helena, Constantine's mother, is said to have been especially eager to erect memorials and buildings at holy sites throughout the country. Her fervor must have grated on Jewish nerves as much as the massive statues of Stalin erected throughout Eastern Europe must irritate the inhabitants of the countries in which the statues are found.

Eventually, Palestine was taken over by the Muslims; in 640 the caliph Omar was master. The centuries of Muslim domination saw cultivated valleys become swamps, hill slopes given over to Bedouin grazers, and the highlands deforested. In the ninth century Egypt gained control, only to lose it to the Crusaders in 1099. After less than one hundred years, the Latin Kingdom of Jerusalem expired, to be replaced by the rule of the Mamelukes until 1516, when the Ottoman Turks defeated the Mamelukes. After World War I, the British acquired the area as a mandate of the League of Nations, and, according to the terms of the Balfour Declaration in 1917, Palestine was marked as the place for the setting up of a Jewish national state.

Immigrations of overseas Jews into Palestine began during the administration of the Ottoman Turks. Of greatest importance in the increase of Jewish population during this period were the Sephardic immigrants from the Iberian Peninsula in the thirteenth century. Among them were the famous poet Judah Halevi and the great philosopher Maimonides. Also during this period, Don Joseph Nasi, the Duke of Naxos, acquired a charter from Suleiman the Magnificent granting him lands in Tiberias, where he set up a refuge for persecuted Jews. He also planted mulberry trees and attempted to develop sericulture, but since at that time the silk industry was a virtual monopoly of the Italians, pirates from Malta attacked ships bringing Jews to Tiberias and captured the people and sold them into slavery. For this reason, the number of actual immigrants was smaller than Nasi had hoped it would be. In short, immigration of Jews to Palestine was never totally interrupted, and it began to pick up tempo around 1870 with heavy immigrations from Europe. It is clear, then, that for centuries Palestine has been a goal for the Jews.

It amazes me that the Japanese insist that the trouble in Palestine is a fight among races and for the sake of land claims. In refutation, I must first point out that Palestine is today very sparsely populated. There is plenty of land for everyone. Along the east bank of the Jordan is a great deal of undeveloped land that could be used for agriculture. The mountains are largely exposed and unused. As far as the claim that the conflict is a racial one is concerned, I must hasten to say that even during the British Mandate, Jews and Arabs fought together against the supposedly Nazi-affiliated Mufti of Jerusalem, Haji Amin Al-Husseini, and his private army. They also worked together when necessary to counter Mandate authorities. Even today, Arabs remaining in Israel are represented in the Israeli parliament. Another non-Jewish group, the Druses, are one of the Jews' closest allies, and in 1951 many of them received written thanks for their contribution to Israeli independence.

Having shown that the conflict is neither racial nor a matter of land, I shall use a simple illustration to prove what it is all about. Suppose that in imperial Russia a band of Jews had moved onto the estate of a great landowner and had set up a kolkhoz, or better still, a model Jewish kibbutz. What would have happened? The answer is easy: the landowner would have banded his serfs together into a small army or police force and would have done all in his power to crush the kibbutz as quickly as possible. On the other hand, suppose the Jews had bought land on which to establish their farm. In such a case, quarrels over boundaries might have grown into a battle over land; and discrimination against the Jews for daring to own land at all might have produced a racial crisis. But such would never be the outcome of a situation in which the Jews merely built their collective farms on another person's land. In short, then, the current state of affairs is the result of a conflict between a feudal, landowner-dominated society— such as may be found in Iraq—supported by oil revenues and military forces and a modern, communal-oriented society represented by such an institution as the Israeli kibbutz.

The State of Israel is really a federation between the Jews and the Arabs. The two national languages are Hebrew and Arabic, and government proceedings and court decisions are made public in both. Arabs make up about one-tenth of the membership of the Israel labor federation, and they account for the same percentage of public officers and policemen. Moreover, there is not an Arab living in Israel who seriously supports the doctrines advocated by Egypt, especially those advanced by the late President Nasser. If there were such Arabs, the State of Israel would collapse tomorrow. But should this happen, the Arabs would find themselves serfs without rights, working twice as hard and realizing about one-quarter of their present income. Obviously, they see no profit in that, and for this reason Israel, while containing a fairly large number of her own Arabs, is able to survive surrounded by hundreds of thousands of other Arabs. Military force is not the nation's only defense. The key to the Sinai front is Hebron and Bethlehem, both inhabited almost entirely by Arabs. If these people decided to follow the lead of Egypt, the Sinai front would collapse immediately. But no one is worried about this eventuality because the war is a battle between two systems, and the Arabs in Israel know that they are better off than they would be under the alternative social structure.

Generally speaking, the Japanese are easy to convince. When they see themselves in error, they usually admit their mistake and change their views accordingly. But some

Japanese intellectuals are suprisingly stubborn persons; once they take to an idea no amount of refutation will move them from their positions. As a case in point, and another example of how Jewish ways are often misconstrued in Japan, I would cite the common interpretation of the *lex talionis*. Japanese are prone to regard the famous "eye for an eye" doctrine as an incitation to vengeance when attacked. But this is not the case. Rather, the lex talionis calls for equal justice for all, not for an insensate revenge. For example, in Leviticus we read:

"He who kills a man shall be put to death. He who kills a beast shall make it good, life for life. When a man causes a disfigurement in his neighbor, as he has done it shall be done to him, fracture for fracture, eye for eye, tooth for tooth. . . ." (Lev. 24: 17–20)

And in Deuteronomy:

"A single witness shall not prevail against a man for any crime or for any wrong in connection with any offense that he has committed; only on the evidence of two witnesses, or of three witnesses, shall a charge be sustained. If a malicious witness arises against any man to accuse him of wrongdoing, then both parties to the dispute shall appear before the Lord, before the priests and the judges who are in office in those days; the judges shall inquire diligently, and if the witness is a false witness and has accused his brother falsely then you shall do to him as he had meant to do to his brother; so you shall purge the evil from the midst of you. And the rest shall hear, and fear, and shall never again commit any such evil among you. Your eye shall not pity; it shall be life for life, eye for eye, tooth for tooth, hand for hand, foot for foot." (Deut. 19: 15–21)

It seems to me impossible to construe these passages to mean that one can or must take revenge when one is offended. On the contrary, they say that one must make retribution for one's wrongdoings in a manner equivalent to the kind and gravity of the offense. That many Japanese fail to understand this is but another of the blind spots that occur when they look outside their own society.

In this chapter I have recorded a few of the misconceptions the Japanese have about Jews. They are not alone in their misreadings of Jewish culture, whether ancient or modern, but the errors cited here reflect a Japanese propensity—which I will discuss later—to make judgments too quickly and too easily about outsiders. In this, the Japanese are somewhat misguided optimists.

13. Abacus and Formula Thinking

IN JAPANESE RESTAURANTS, PARSLEY is on every plate, but no one ever eats it. Once at a conference between Israeli leaders and some Japanese financial experts, simple sandwiches were served as light refreshment. After everyone had finished the snacks, the Jews noticed that on each of the white plates lined up in front of the Japanese members of the party the parsley garnish remained untouched, whereas some of the Jews had eaten theirs. With typical reference to rule, the puzzled Jews asked the Japanese if they had some law against eating parsley. But of course this could not be true, for in such a case, parsley would not have been served at all. Could it be that coincidentally all of the Japanese belonged to an organization that forbids the consumption of parsley? Perhaps all of the men happened to dislike the vegetable.

None of these suppositions, however, is true, although the correct answer is very simple.

The Japanese require trimming, or the softening addition of a garnish, which they never attempt to put to more practical use. The garnish effect alone is sufficient. For example, one of the luxury foods in Japan is *sashimi,* sliced raw fish, which is invariably served with ornamental leaves or other pleasing additions that are later thrown away. Unlike the salads that Westerners design to be both attractive and nutritious, the ornamental dainties served with sashimi are unrelated to food value. It might be argued that since the fish is the important thing the sensible way to serve it would be unadorned. Indeed, from the Jewish standpoint, the presence of detracting elements on the plate prevents the diner from savoring fine foods to the fullest measure. In short, the content, not the accouterment, is the important thing. The Japanese, however, do not agree; and I believe that one of the reasons they do not read Hebrew literature is that although the content is of the purest gold, the container is clay and ungarnished into the bargain. The Japanese find this bare and unappealing. In theory, if the gold of the content is pure, no handsome serving dish or elegant trimming can increase and no mean vessel can reduce its value as gold. But this is theory, and as I have said, the Japanese generally reject theorizing. In short, they require a garnish element, no matter how excellent the fare. This desire is reflected in aspects of Japanese life other than culinary ones.

The young lady who studies English literature at a university is garnishing herself to become a bride. The practical uselessness of what she learns is beside the point. Furthermore, it is only natural that she not flaunt her education, since it is fundamentally no more than trimming. As a matter of fact, other Japanese would find her very distasteful should she treat her educational finery as a source of pride. On a wider scale, universities themselves garnish society, since they provide individual human beings with appealing, if not always practical or profitable, ornaments.

Perhaps the largest and most interesting group of people whose function is similar to that of trimmings on plates of food is that of the professional critics. I shall deal with them in some detail because their garnish function bridges the gap between the traditional Japanese way of thinking and the Western ideas that the people of Japan have been importing for the past century.

Japan has more professional critics than any nation in the world, and the subject matter that they criticize extends over a surprising range. In the West the critic is generally confined to comments on and evaluations of artistic matters: the theater, motion pictures, books, paintings, sculpture, and so on. But in Japan critics on medicine, economics, and other nonartistic fields abound. Even when their readers are not as numerous as in Western countries, Japanese critics exert important influences on national life in all things from chopsticks to fancy automobiles. Oddly enough, most of them are armchair philosophers although I prefer to call them poolsiders.

At many swimming pools some persons, seated comfortably in deck chairs beside the water, make informed comments on all the fine points of swimming though they themselves would scream for help from the lifeguard if they so much as fell into the shallow end. These are the poolsiders. In Japan, it is not unusual to find a man whose own business has gone bankrupt serving as economic critic for an important periodical. Having taken the plunge into business and nearly perished, such men have retired to the deck chairs: they have become poolsiders. But far from despising such a man, many Japanese maintain that he probably has very interesting things to say. As a Jew disagreeing with this viewpoint, I sometimes object: "But a man who can't swim also can't tell another person how to swim. And if this is so, only a critic who knows what he is talking about is worth listening to." To this my Japanese friends reply that in a sense I am correct but that critics, whether successes or failures in their lines, deserve to be heard. "Well," I go on in this imaginary colloquy, "if you take the bankrupt economic critic's advice and as a result follow him into bankruptcy, is it his fault?" The reply I can expect to receive is this: "Such things may happen, but when they do, it is the fault of the person who blindly follows the critic's advice. After all, no one makes him heed what the writer says."

All of this leads to the conclusion that critics are not responsible for what they say. Because I see a strong connection between freedom and responsibility, to me the lack of one suggests an impairment of the other. On the contrary, the Japanese contend that it would be an encroachment on the critic's freedom to hold him responsible for his words. If what he says offends, it ought to be ignored. But he must be allowed to say what he likes. This attitude seems excessively disinterested, but the phrase "Let him say what he likes" recurs with such frequency in Japanese conversations that I am convinced that it signifies much more than its superficial meaning.

When the Old Testament says "Hear, O Israel," it means that Israel is to hear, understand, and obey. The Japanese sometimes obey what they hear—or read—but because they do not believe in infallible authorities, they always select what to heed and what to disregard on the basis of the exigencies of the situation. Consequently, critics may write sense or nonsense; the Japanese will choose what they need and discard the rest. This attitude makes possible the existence of multitudes of critics in Japan and makes my objections to them seem immature and frivolous.

To pursue this point a little further, I might ask this question. If the Japanese can and do select the good from the bad in what critics say, why are so many critics needed? Is it not conceivable that over a period of time, Japanese selection would weed out the worthless, leaving only the astute and valuable? The answer is no, because of the nature of the Japanese critic's role, which I can metaphorically describe in two ways.

First, the critic in Japan is like a fashion model. It is sometimes said of these slender ladies that they wear their fine trappings with such ease and grace that they might have been born in them. The fact is, of course, that their shoes, gloves, and gowns have been designed and made by someone else. The models wear them elegantly but lack the ability to produce them. Critics, intellectuals, and men of culture in Japan often resemble fashion models in that they deck their brains in the latest Western ideas and do so with such consummate skill that they seem to have been thinking that way since their births. Again, like models, when the fashion changes, they shed the old and don the new, filling the costume-change interim with various entertainments. In this way they manage to stay on stage all of the time. But their function is display; they have no responsibility for the effects of their philosophical apparel. A woman may buy the fashionable long skirt displayed by a model. But if, while wearing it, the customer trips and breaks her leg, it is not the model's fault. Similarly, the Japanese critic is not to blame if someone blindly follows his borrowed Western ideas to bankruptcy and ruin. Japanese critics, college professors, and others who make public pronouncements probably have at-home wardrobes of ideas too, but the proper way to interpret their fashion-show philosophies—and every Japanese of sense knows this—is to accept the acceptable and reject the rest. In short, this is the meaning of "Let him say what he likes."

The second metaphor that illuminates the part the critic plays in Japan is that of the garnish. As I have said, Hebrew literature is too unadorned to be readily welcomed by the Japanese. The same thing may be said for many of the Western ideas the Japanese have adopted, but it has been the critic who has acted as the garnishing element converting bare ideas into palatable commodities. In order to explain how he achieved this, I must first explain why such a role is necessary in the light of the disparate Western and Japanese approaches toward what I shall call subconscious education.

Children willy-nilly learn certain attitudes and philosophies from their parents by absorption. No matter how much they may rebel against parental authority, their very rebellion constitutes a kind of parent-inspired education in that it at least signifies awareness of the things the parents stand for. It is unfair to ask a people to explain the workings of their subconscious education, because they are by and large unaware of them. My experience, however, allows me to know how different subconscious education is in the cases of the Japanese and the Jews. My parents were stubborn orthodox Jews, but I was born in Japan. All of our neighbors were Japanese, and I went to a Japanese primary school. For these reasons, I knew what kinds of things young Japanese learned, though in my own home, where I was the only person who spoke Japanese, I learned quite different things.

If individual children inevitably fall under the formative influence of their immediate environment, a whole nation too can be molded in many respects by the cumulative national experience. In the case of the Japanese, two important parts of traditional subconscious education have had far-reaching effects on the way of thinking of the whole people. One of those has to do with training in numbers and the other with lack of training in words.

In the West the adding machine came into being after long centuries in which calculations were done on paper. In Japan, however, the abacus was widely used to perform such operations long before the importation of Arabic numerals and written mathematics of which they are the basis. So widely used is the abacus even today that department store clerks and many other people whose work involves a certain amount of figuring consider it an essential tool of their trades. Foreign visitors to Japanese stores are usually startled by the speed and accuracy with which salesgirls add up sums on their abacuses. Though of course today Arabic numerals and mathematics are important aspects of all formal education, the tradition of the abacus persists in the national experience as a vital part of subconscious education. And as such, it has played a role in conditioning the Japanese way of thinking.

A mathematician working with written numbers must concentrate his whole mind. He must be careful and persevering in his work. His mind must be filled with what he is doing and must never wander. A Japanese working with the abacus must adopt the opposite approach. Instead of thinking consciously, he must rid his mind of awareness of the problem and, becoming almost absent-minded, allow his fingers to fly over the beads until the correct answer emerges. And the Japanese think of the answer precisely as emerging of itself instead of being the outcome of a conscious process of calculation. An archer must allow the arrow some life of its own; if he aims too deliberately, he spoils his shot. A ballet dancer forgets everything during a performance and, riding on the music, simply dances. These psychological states and that of the Japanese working with the abacus resemble the thought-less condition that is the core of the teaching of Zen Buddhism.

I have a friend who is so expert with the abacus that he does not require the physical presence of the device itself to do highly complicated calculations. It is true that he must consciously conjure up his mental abacus; but once he has done so, he proceeds to calculate with it in the virtually absent-minded state required. His special feat of mental calculation is difficult and rare, but the surprising thing to the Westerner is probably not so much his unusual talent as the very idea of calculations made thought-lessly. Nevertheless, answers of the greatest accuracy emerge from the abacus. If verification of a sum is necessary, it cannot be done by checking back figure by figure, since there is nothing written to check. Instead one must either redo the sum oneself or have another person do it. If the answers agree, they are correct.

All Japanese children are trained in numbers, at any rate in the use of the abacus. Oddly enough, however, no Japanese children are subjected to similar training in the employment of words. When a mother tells her child to say something correctly, she is referring not to grammar, but to the intricate levels of courtesy involved in speaking Japanese. Once a young Japanese girl remarked to me in a tone of surprise that Latin, which she was studying at the time, reminded her more of mathematics than of language. In order to understand her feeling, it is imperative to realize that the Japanese language is totally unrelated to such inflected languages as those of the Indo-European group. Instead of consciously selecting from a wide range of possibilities to express a fixed grammatical number, case, or tense, the Japanese add words in what is called an agglutinative process. Of course, there are rules to follow in Japanese, but in comparison with the elaborate, almost mathematical formula-style grammars of languages like classical Latin or modern Russian, these rules play a less important part.

What does count for a great deal, however, is the way things are said; that is, the attitude of the speaker, his intonation, and his regard for matters of courtesy. When a mother corrects her child's language in Japan these are the things she has in mind. In other words, speaking in broad general terms, I might say that the Indo-European languages strive to express content with clarity as a result of adherence to prescribed grammatical rules. Japanese, on the other hand, prefers to concentrate on form.

I might illustrate my meaning by referring to one of the dialogues of Plato. The dialogue as a literary form is conspicuously absent in Japanese letters. The late novelist

Yukio Mishima once commented on this and remarked that even were the Japanese to attempt literature in the dialogue style, it would necessarily be limited to satire. In the *Crito,* Socrates, on the eve of his death, advocates obedience to the law and refutes Crito, who hopes to convince Socrates to flee from prison. At the opening of the dialogue Socrates is reclining, as is only natural, since it is night. Nowhere does Plato say that Socrates arose, adjusted himself in a dignified manner, and proceeded to discourse in an attitude suitable to the gravity of his words. It is the clear reasoning of what he says, not how he says it, that matters; and in all likelihood he remained in a reclining position until the conclusion of the discussion. But Japanese language training is based on the idea that attitude, deportment, and above all accurate selection of the courteous forms suited to the occasion are of the utmost importance. For a person of consequence to deliver a significant talk in a careless, let alone reclining, posture would violate decorum and, from the Japanese viewpoint, be as serious a fault as ungrammatical language. A learned discourse delivered by a conservative college professor or the firebrand arguments of radical students shouted over loudspeakers in front of train stations employ the same level of courteous language thought appropriate for a speaker addressing a group of people. In short, the form remains constant, though the content may vary dramatically.

In addition to the difference in emphasis on content and form, the nature of words themselves in the West and in Japan are very different. In languages like Hebrew, French, Greek, or Russian, words are invariably bound to some concrete meaning. I think of the individual word in these languages as a cone with a secure base of definite meaning and an abstract or associative pinnacle. No matter how abstract the Western speaker may wish to be, he cannot divest the individual word of its concrete content. The Japanese, on the other hand, can do exactly that, with the result that their words sometimes resemble spheres devoid of concrete meaning. The nature of their words enables them to do a number of amazing feats of abstract writing and speaking almost totally devoid of real content or laden with bewildering abstract contradictions. This is especially notable in translations and commentaries on the Bible. Japanese specialists in these matters often say things like: "The virgin birth and the Resurrection cannot be called true, but it is a fact that they are a kind of truth." In translation such a statement is ludicrous, whereas when spoken in Japanese it seems to make a sense of its own.

To this point I have said that the Japanese always prefer things garnished instead of served unornamented, no matter how excellent the thing itself. I have also shown that, instead of being a mathematically precise language oriented toward the attainment of clarity of expression, Japanese tends to abstraction and to an emphasis on correctness of form in place of lucidity. Before leaving the nature of the Japanese language, however, I must hasten to correct the impression that it is a tool of such fuzziness and inconvenience as to be useless in conveying ordinary information. This patently is not the case, for if the language were that impractical, Japanese society could not have reached its present level of sophistication. On the contrary, the Japanese language suits the needs of the Japanese people to perfection because it requires the same abacus-style thinking that I have discussed in connection with mathematics. Their words, as round as the beads of an abacus, require unconscious, untrammeled manipulation. Just as an abacus operator who thinks too much about what he does virtually paralyzes his fingers and makes his work impossible, so the manipulator of the Japanese language cannot afford to get bogged down in the grammatical niceties on which inflected languages depend for meaning.

In metaphorical terms, the mental abacus of my talented friend represents the Japanese way of thinking. In both the West and in Japan, words are the raw material of thought. The Westerner martials his store of words in grammatical patterns similar in some respects to algebraic formulas. The structure of his language and centuries of training in logic-oriented thought have made it imperative for him to do so. But the Japanese uses a verbal abacus over which his mind dances, like the fingers of the person working with the real abacus. His words are perfectly adapted to this kind of thinking because they are round, ball-like objects that roll about in disorder if one attempts to arrange them in Western formula-style patterns.

After the Meiji Restoration, the Japanese imported Western ideas in massive doses, and the influx has not ceased yet. But if Japanese words do not lend themselves to the expression of these ideas, some kind of interpreter becomes essential. This brings me back to the poolsider, the critic, and the commentator. I have said that they are fashion models parading in borrowed finery, but they are also the garnish that makes unpalatable lumps of ideas more appealing. And most important, they are the people whose duty it is to arrange Western formula thoughts in a way that is comprehensible to abacus-style thinkers. For such a role, originality is unessential. The bankrupt economics expert can present borrowed ideas in an abacus-style conversion that makes sense to his readers. The skillful abacus operator works unconsciously; he is unable to explain the process by means of which he arrives at his answers. Similarly, though incapable of saying how he does it, a person with a certain knowledge of Western thoughts can convert them into abacus thinking and perform the reverse process, as well. Such a person is not a Western formula-style thinker any more than a Westerner who lived in Japan for a only few years would ever become truly proficient in the abacus. Both are part of the unconscious educational patterns of two different worlds of thought. In order for a person from one world to master the patterns of the other, he would have to begin his education, both conscious and—if it were possible—unconscious, all over again. People who do no more than interpret the rules of one system in terms of the other, however, fulfill a valuable function: they can give the abacus experts hints that might detonate totally novel ways of using this calculating device. This is the most important task of the poolsider, and it does not matter that his work—like the garnish on a plate of sashimi—may be destined for the trashcan.

In Japan today, the old abacus educational system has given ground to the new formula one. The most successful modern Japanese are the ones who, having thoroughly mastered the abacus way of doing things, can verify its results by means of the formula-style process of deliberate and conscious thought. Such people are not numerous. At the other end of the scale are the failures who master neither system. Often these are the people who have traveled abroad to study and while there have lost their own national personalities without acquiring new ones of any significance. I know a university teacher who falls into this category. Since he is skillful at a foreign language, he interprets for politicians and men of businessaffairs. Once he said to me that anyone who interprets and thus meets intelligent people from other countries loses sympathy with the weakheadedness of Japanese businessmen. While in middle school, I read of a man who visited a foreign country where he learned a new way of walking. So well did he learn that when he returned to his homeland he found that he had forgotten his own native stride. Unable to use his newly acquired gait and no longer capable of walking as his countrymen did, he was compelled to crawl. My interpreter-teacher is in this predicament. He has abandoned his own intellectual background for a foreign education and is now an intellectual cripple in his own land. Fortunately his position in the world is neither influential nor responsible, and the damage he can do is slight. There have been instances in the past, however, when people of authority and power have shared his ailment, with disastrous results for their subordinates and superiors alike. Oddly enough, among cases that I know, the people causing the trouble generally managed to come out either unscathed or in improved circumstances.

The long and short of the matter, however, is that no one—not a Jew, nor a Japanese, nor a European Christian —can consciously cancel the subconscious part of his education. For this reason, most Japanese will go on following neither the pure abacus-style nor the unadulterated formula-style of thinking. Instead they will use the latter to verify the former and thus make new discoveries that will ultimately find expression in society. The side by side operation of these fundamentally irreconcilable ways of thinking has already taken a toll in victims. Some of the sacrifices have been people who simply fell by the wayside, unable to do anything because of the confusion born of the conflict between the two patterns. Others have suffered because of a similar inability on the part of people in authority. Nonetheless, in the light of conditions as they exist now, it seems that the Japanese will not alter their position of balance between an old deeply rooted tradition and a new philosophy requiring semantic conversion for the sake of comprehensibility.

My friend who can operate the abacus mentally would deride any attempts to convince him that his imaginary calculating device does not exist. Perhaps it is intangible, but it has a very real existence. Moreover, it can give accurate answers to problems, in that way can influence all aspects of daily life, and finally can be the source from which judgments evolve. Of course, I am talking about the abacus as a symbol of the entire Japanese way of thinking as it manifests itself in pragmatism, conformity to the exigencies of the moment, and preference for forms with highly varying contents. Indeed in this sense the abacus does exist.

In a very similar way, the Jew would refuse to countenance attempts to prove that because the physical existence of God and the Law cannot be demonstrated they are mere fictions. For the Jews, God is the abacus producing answers in the form of the Law, which is immutable and definitive. My abacus specialist feels no need to announce that he believes in an invisible calculating device whose answering powers he knows. Unlike the Christians, the Jews do not need to assert their belief in an invisible God. The abacus principle, like that of humanity, is shared by all Japanese to the extent that they are often unaware of

it. Consequently they have never been called on to suffer
for holding this belief. The Jewish experience, in this as in
many other phases of life and history, is different. The
Christians, like fakes in the presence of the true thing, have
screamed loud and long that they believe in God. Yet they
have demonstrated the weakness of their faith by persecut-
ing the Jews, whose faith is too strong to need proclamation.

The concept behind the abacus principle for every Japanese is humanity. This is not a physical flesh-and-blood
humanity, but a guiding idea, intangible yet very real, as
are God and the Law from the standpoint of the Jews. Interestingly enough this kind of humanity does not exist for
the Westerner, just as the Western and Hebraic concepts of
God do not exist for the Japanese. Furthermore, Westerners can no more comprehend a world based on this
concept of humanity than they can grasp the abacus way
of thinking.

*   *   *

Bookshops in Tokyo are lined with volumes containing
Japanese writers' impressions of America and of various
European countries. Each work claims to be an accurate
record of the facts of life about another country, because
the writers, holding to the naive belief that objectivity is in
the mind of the observer, ignore distortions that arise from
uncommon backgrounds and divergent cultural training.
This belief is nonsense, especially when one is comparing
Western nations with Japan.

For instance, cash registers are sold in both America and
Japan, but the reasons salesmen put forth to persuade
prospective customers to buy are entirely different. Deeply
convinced that humanity is sinful, Americans consider it

evil to put temptation in a man's way. Therefore, an American salesman would expect to sell more cash registers by saying that his product is guaranteed to keep the clerks in a shop honest by making it impossible for them to filch from the till. If a Japanese salesman were to adopt such a line he would probably be out of a job within a week. A shopkeeper once explained to me that all human beings make mistakes—unintentionally—and that the cash register is a convenient way to prevent suspicion of error and a consequent lowering of morale in a shop. (As I have pointed out elsewhere, Japanese are pragmatic but they always strive to preserve harmony in human relations.) The fact of the need for a cash register is the same, but the interpretations of the need reflect quite dissimilar approaches to life.

Unfortunately, many Japanese writing about foreign nations do so in the conviction that close contact breeds mutual understanding in spite of cultural differences. According to this point of view, the world is growing smaller in the age of the jumbo jet and supersonic transport; soon everyone will have come to know each other and will work side by side in harmony. In short, to know is to remove barriers to incomprehension. But I believe this is fallacious, and in closing this book I feel impelled to warn the Japanese that their optimism in this respect is dangerous. For thousands of years the Jews have lived in contact with the gentile populations of the world, and we all know how much mutual understanding that proximity has brought about.

The "weathermark" identifies this book as having been planned, designed, and produced at the Tokyo offices of John Weatherhill, Inc. Book design and typography by Meredith Weatherby. Composed and printed by Kenkyusha, Tokyo. Bound at the Okamoto Binderies, Tokyo. The typeface used is Baskerville, with display type in hand-set Bulmer.